NO LONGER NOMADS

NO LONGER NOMADS
The Sirionó Revisited

by

Allyn MacLean Stearman
University of Central Florida

Hamilton Press

LANHAM • NEW YORK • LONDON

Copyright © 1987 by

Hamilton Press

4720 Boston Way
Lanham, MD 20706

3 Henrietta Street
London WC2E 8LU England

British Cataloging in Publication Information Available

Library of Congress Cataloging in Publication Data

Stearman, Allyn MacLean, 1943-
   No longer nomads.

   Bibliography: p.
   Includes index.
   1. Siriono Indians.   2. Siriono Indians—Cultural
assimilation.   3. Indians of South America—Bolivia—
Cultural assimilation.   4. Stearman, Allyn MacLean,
1943-   . I. Title.
F3320.2.S5S74   1987   305.8'98   86-25672
ISBN 0-8191-5315-X (pbk. : alk. paper)

All Hamilton Press books are produced on acid-free
paper which exceeds the minimum standards set by the National
Historical Publication and Records Commission.

Hamilton Press

Contents

List of Illustrations and Figures

Illustrations:

Figures

Twenty pages of photographs follow page 98.
All sketches and photographs, except where noted, are by the author.

Acknowledgements

I owe a special debt of gratitude to two women who from the beginning had faith that I would not only find the Sirionó, but would return to study them. Their efforts to secure funding for my research in Bolivia in large part made this book possible: Dr. Joan Burr, Director of Sponsored Research at the University of Central Florida, and Dr. Marianne Schmink, Director of the Amazon Research and Training Program at the University of Florida. I would also like to thank those colleagues and anonymous reviewers who took time away from busy schedules to read the manuscript and offer helpful suggestions for its improvement, especially Ida Cook, Ray Crist, Paul Doughty, Dwight Heath, Maxine Margolis, David Stoll, and Charles Wagley. I, of course, take final responsibility for the content.

A special thanks to Betsy Swayne who patiently took scribblings and scraps and rendered them into a manuscript, at times reworking the same page over and over again until we were both satisfied with the result. Judy Goffman edited this and previous works of mine, as always using her skill and perception to turn flagrant abuses of the English language into acceptable prose while at the same time preserving the essence and flavor of the narrative. Lauryn Erndl of Instructional Resources at the University of Central Florida spent many hours working on the maps and graphics that appear here. Her supervisor and my friend, Dorothy Kannon, encouraged me in my attempts to illustrate in pen and ink part of my experience with the Sirionó.

While in Bolivia, I received assistance from Jürgen Riester, a German anthropologist residing there who is involved in the human rights struggle of Native Americans, particularly those in the Bolivian lowlands. For more than twenty years, Father Ray Cowell has opened his doors to me, always graciously providing me with room and board while I stayed in the city of Santa Cruz. His willingness to offer an oasis, a resting place from the stresses of fieldwork, no doubt has contributed to my eagerness to continue to face the rigors of working in the Bolivian *oriente*. Jack and Darlene Anderson welcomed me into their home in Trinidad, providing not only a hospice but fascinating tales of the Sirionó as well. To my husband, Mike, a very fond and heartfelt tribute. He has always understood my need to go off to faraway places to practice the craft of anthropology.

Finally, I would like to express my appreciation to the Sirionó who invited me to travel with them, if only briefly, along their journey of life.

Preface

The question that always comes to anthropologists is why we study, or are even concerned with the exotic, remote, and unimportant people so identified with the discipline. What value can the study of such cultures hold for self-proclaimed advanced, post-industrial societies? Is the life and fate of a few hundred impoverished Indians of any priority in the context of the nuclear age? Surely for most, the Sirionó of the Bolivian tropical frontier are a people only to be appreciated anthropologically. Why they should become the subject matter of books and dozens of scientific articles may be cause for wonderment, but readers of this volume will discover the intricate drama of life that is, to borrow Barbara Tuchman's phrase, a "distant mirror" of our own.

The Sirionó are destined to remain in their unique position in South American ethnology. Allan Holmberg's original book about them, *Nomads of the Long Bow*, now available in its third edition, is one of the few ethnographies to remain in print for so long. Making this all the more remarkable is the fact that Sirionó themselves, living in a rather unpleasant and certainly difficult environment in a state of endemic starvation, exploited and persecuted along an unmanaged frontier were far from being either attractive or easily romanticized by any imagination. According to Holmberg (1969):

> One cannot remain long with the Sirionó without noting that quarreling and wrangling are ubiquitous. (153)

> They accuse each other of not sharing food...and of stealing off into the forest to eat. (154)

> The disputes are settled by wrestling matches and are usually forgotten after the period of drunkenness is over. (156)

Yet, when first published in 1950, *Nomads* quickly became one of the most cited and controversial contributions to the literature for reasons that were evident even to novice students. It was at once a methodological landmark in the annals of ethnography because of the daunting conditions under which the study was conducted. The unpretentious monograph published by the Smithsonian Institution, written in a parsimonious but convincing style succeeded in raising a series of ethnological, ethical, and policy questions that as time would reveal, were of transcendental, even growing importance. These elements account for the fact that 36 years after its original publication, *Nomads of the Long Bow* is still one of the most widely cited ethnographies in the South American and world wide literature and is continually featured as case study material in leading anthropological texts (the most recent example being Wendall Oswalt's *Life Cycles and Lifeways,* Mayfield, 1986).

Of the several issues raised by Holmberg, few have become more significant than that of the context itself: the nature of the Amazonian frontier and the interface of human societies. In 1950, this was one of the remotest places on earth, a place where Holmberg hoped to study unaculturated, uncontacted aboriginal peoples. Not only did he discover that the Sirionó were intermittently influenced by outsiders—ranchers, missionaries, colonists—but that they were usually brutally exploited even in "benign" and well-intentioned contexts. He discovered that the Sirionó, like other native American populations (as we have increasingly come to realize) had been deeply affected by disease and depopulation although in his day, few if any scholars understood the enormity of the demographic and cultural impact of such events. This affected Holmberg's analysis of Sirionó technological primitiveness and social organization significantly in view of the fact that he attempted to explain the reasons for the anomalies he found.

Another of the important areas in which Holmberg's work stimulated interest was in the frontier and the drama of life it provided. Between Holmberg's lines of ethnographic data appears his concern over the conditions under which the Sirionó struggled to survive. Indeed, the theoretical topic motivating the study was an examination of the effects of endemic and periodic hunger on social, psychological, and cultural life; a theme suggested to him at Yale as he studied there in the late 1930s. Holmberg's interests were composed of a strong mix of Malinowskian functionalism, George Murdock's cross-cultural comparative approach, theories of culture and personality espoused by Ralph Linton, John Dollard and others, and the South American ethnological orientation of Alfred Métraux.

Imbued with a strong sense of scientific purpose and an exceptional research design which actually sought to *test* hypotheses in field conditions (a true novelty for the ethnographer of Holmberg's day), he was poised to raise other questions as well. These were ones which attended the impact of Euro-American industrial technology and society on such peoples as the Sirionó, engulfing them in exploitive dependency or destroying them. His study also raised in his mind the problem still challenging anthropologists: what can or should we do about such conditions? His own experiences with the Sirionó left him with feelings of great ambivalence and concern.

Once he left the Sirionó to write up his data in the post World War II years, Holmberg never had the opportunity of returning, spending the rest of his career in Andean research and applied anthropology. While teaching at the National University of San Marcos in Lima (1947–8) he helped train a generation of Peruvian anthropologists, among them Mario Vázquez, José

Matos Mar, Oscar Nuñez del Prado, and José María Argüedas whom he directed in field research. Later he made it possible for over 90 students from Peru and the United States to work on the Vicos research and development project from 1951 through 1964. I was one of those.

In 1960 Cornell, Harvard, and Columbia Universities had a summer program for undergraduates sponsored by the Carnegie Corporation for which I was field director in the Peruvian highlands. Allan arrived in July and recruited all to pay a short research visit to the coastal town of Viru where he first worked in 1946-7. Riding on the train from the Callejón de Huaylas down the Andes to the port of Chimbote, Allan was sitting behind me and all were engaged in lively discussion of the passing scene, with Holmberg contributing anecdotal comments, comparing the "rigors" of our field experience to his with the Sirionó. Summarizing, he concluded that I was the only one who evidenced the consequences of similar ordeals, judging by my haircut which resembled the ragged unisex style of the Sirionó. That was the closest I ever got to the forest nomads.

While in Lima in 1964 Holmberg asked me to accompany him to the Beni to find and visit the Sirionó people he had studied. Enthusiasm over this prospect was short-lived however: Allan suddenly fell ill with appendicitis complicated by peritonitis, and barely survived the ordeal. The trip to Bolivia was out of the question. This painful episode came after his serious bout with tuberculosis in 1961-2, a disease he had surely contracted somewhere in his South American sojourns. The appendicitis was followed by a terminal struggle with cancer in 1966.

Although I never heard him say so directly, Holmberg suggested on several occasions that it was this confrontation with the exploitation of the Sirionó along the Beni frontier which fully aroused his scientific and humanitarian commitment to applied anthropology. Allan was deeply moved by such conditions and confident that anthropologists had the skill and knowledge, indeed, the obligation, to initiate corrective action where the moment was right. His experimental attempts to aid and alter Sirionó circumstances were limited, tentative and in the end, unsuccessful.

Nevertheless, such a time came at Hacienda Vicos, Ancash, 3,000 meters high in the north central Peruvian Andes far from tropical forest tangle where the Sirionó endured. With Peruvian colleagues, Holmberg began the Cornell-Peru Project in 1951-2, a pioneering effort to apply anthropological approaches to end peonage, achieve a model for successful agrarian reform and create the basis for positive changes among impoverished Quechua highlanders, thus resolving the Andean "Indian problem" without doing away with Indians. It was a project which again placed Holmberg's contributions at the forefront of modern anthropology and precipitated waves of controversy over the possibilities for applied anthropology.

xi

My own contact with Holmberg came as a result of this latter work at Vicos, when Cornell University offered the only program anywhere in Applied Anthropology. As a student in his classes, I was captivated with Allan's low-keyed, thoughtful approach to problems in anthropology: his material was interestingly presented, his bold analyses were rooted in and legitimized by extensive field experience that students recognized as authoritative. The result was that Holmberg's seminars and classes were packed with students drawn from a wide range of disciplines, literally from anthropology to zoology. In 1959, a count revealed that he served on some 56 graduate committees around the campus! It was all too typical of him as someone once complained, "he never could say no to the students."

Allyn Stearman comes to this study as a distant academic descendent in the extensive lineage which Holmberg founded. She not only studied with me as one of Allan's students, but her career in Bolivia has long been focused on the same frontier. She was first there as a Peace Corps volunteer, then as a small farm operator, and finally as an anthropological researcher. She has that special "feel" for the region that translates into authority. The idea of restudying the Sirionó seemed to her not only a logical and important thing to do, but that she could do it. To others, her boldness in attempting such a difficult restudy parallels Holmberg's audacity in the first.

Stearman's account of ethnographic rediscovery in a land of bizarre ironies, human tragedy, hospitality and altruism, and amazing encounters, anecdotally unfolds with wit and sensitivity. Her genius for telling this anthropological saga draws the reader to insights that take us deep into the evolving Amazonian frontier of cultural conflict, despoiled nature and struggling people. As she retraces Holmberg's legendary trail, Stearman not only plunges into an examination of the problems he described, but is miraculously able to build directly on Holmberg's work in their resolution. Even after 40 years the people remembered the anthropologist "Olmber" well, as Stearman, like a detective, meets them one by one and they tell her of life and fate in this rag-tag hinterland of the contemporary world. They are also going to remember his successor, an adventurous "gringa" anthropologist who knew how to ask the right questions, eat the food, chase army ants, sleep in hammocks, wade the jungle streams and mud and as Allan Holmberg did, left behind a trail of friends that someday another might follow. In the meantime, she has given us a book to match the adventure and discovery.

Paul L. Doughty
University of Florida

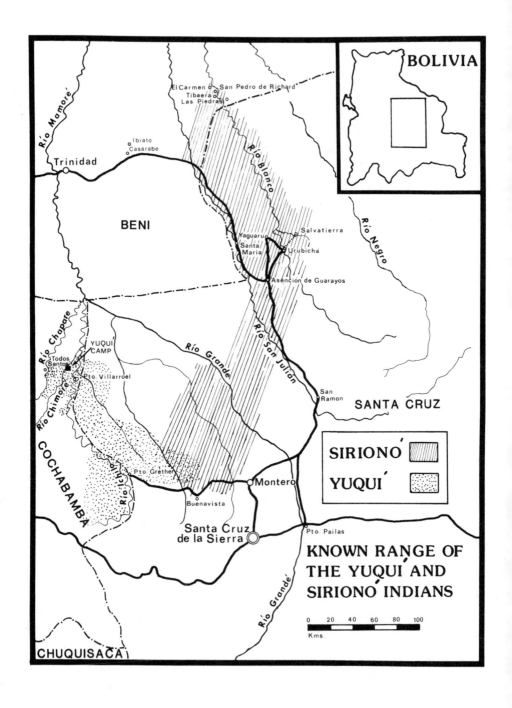

Part
One

The Sirionó are a group of semi-nomadic aborigines inhabiting an extensive tropical forest area, of about 200 miles square, between latitudes 13° and 17° S. and longitudes 63° and 65° W., in northern and eastern Bolivia. The name applied to these Indians is not of their own origin. They refer to themselves simply as *mbia* or "people." But as they have been called Sirionó since first contact, and have been thus designated in the literature, I shall use the term.

—Allan Holmberg
Nomads of the Long Bow

ONE
Chapter 1

Years ago, when the suggestion that I restudy the Sirionó was casually made, I just as casually rejected it. But the idea haunted me, like some unfinished business in my life. The idea began in 1973 when I was walking across campus at the University of Florida with Bill Carter, chairman of my doctoral committee, discussing topics for my dissertation research. Because I had worked as a Peace Corps volunteer in eastern Bolivia, he assumed, correctly, that I would want to return to this area to gather data for my doctoral thesis.

"You know," he said, "you are the ideal person to tackle a restudy of the Sirionó. I don't think anyone has ever gone back to do any follow-up work since Holmberg's classic study. You have experience in the lowlands and no doubt would be able to adapt quite well to the Sirionó region."

I was flattered by his confidence in me, but I also knew exactly what he meant by "adapting." Although it had been several years since I had read *Nomads of the Long Bow*, Allan Holmberg's account of his 1940–41 fieldwork among the Sirionó, I retained a few vivid memories of the book. The Beni province where the Sirionó were located was one of the most inaccessible areas of Bolivia. Holmberg also had suffered numerous debilitating illnesses throughout his fieldwork. In fact, one of his former students, Paul Doughty, had once remarked during a lecture that the Sirionó experience no doubt had contributed to Holmberg's early death at the age of fifty-six. Besides, I had listened to enough stories about the Beni while in Bolivia to convince me that this project was not for me. I had a two-year-old son and, by the time I was ready to go overseas, a newborn daughter to consider in my plans for fieldwork. Perhaps some other time but not now.

I completed my dissertation on another topic, joined the faculty at the University of Central Florida, and settled into the routine duties of academe. But the Sirionó would edge in on me at unexpected moments: a mention in a textbook or a reference in a Latin American anthology or a journal article. One day in 1981, I decided it was time to confront the Sirionó. I don't know what triggered this decision—perhaps restlessness—but once I decided to restudy the Sirionó, I was committed to the project.

My first problem was to determine if in fact the Sirionó had remained unstudied all these years, as Bill Carter had suggested. A lengthy literature search brought me close to *persona non grata* at our Interlibrary Loan office. I wrote to colleagues in Bolivia to inquire about any new data that might have appeared there. Slowly, materials began to arrive, and I was encouraged to see that it all seemed to be based on Holmberg's study. Then a small book and a photocopy of an article arrived from Bolivia, both recent and purporting to offer "new findings." While the publications presented what technically could be called new data, none was current. They were simply recollections of elderly *mestizos* who had known Sirionó during the same period Holmberg was in Bolivia.

One of these studies had an appendix with recent photographs of nude Indians, reportedly Sirionó, taken at the Franciscan mission of Salvatierra. Since this mission had been established in the 1930s, it was inconceivable that after almost fifty years of acculturation, anyone would go unclothed. Upon closer inspection, I discovered that, without exception, the few women appearing in these pictures were fully dressed and the men bore the unmistakable tan marks of shirt-sleeves. The photos of the nude men had obviously been staged. But why this deception? As I reviewed the materials I was receiving, a curious image of the Sirionó began to emerge. In the United States, the lack of additional field data had led to ongoing discussions of Sirionó kinship, subsistence, technology, adaptation, and other subjects, all necessarily derived from Holmberg's study. In Bolivia, publications dealing with the Sirionó were largely a reflection of U.S. interests. Both situations conspired to create the myth of the Sirionó as a people still living in a precontact state. Worse yet, their value as a topic for study, even for present-day researchers, appeared to be tied to that long-vanished era of forest nomadism. This realization further encouraged me that it was time for a new approach.

Before launching plans for a research project dealing with the current situation of the Sirionó, I needed additional background data. I wanted to know more about Holmberg and his work among the Sirionó and gain some insight into the history of the ethnography itself. Also, there was the question of the early effects of acculturation. Since Holmberg's ethnography was basically a study of Sirionó aboriginal culture, only brief mention was made of the acculturation process occurring at the time.

Paul Doughty suggested I first try Holmberg's field notes and helped me to contact Laura Holmberg, Allan Holmberg's widow. She agreed to retrieve his Sirionó journals. I flew to Ithaca, New York, where I spent several days reading Holmberg's field notes. They were a mixture of empirical ethnographic data and personal observations. I found little in the data sections that had not been eventually published. However, the accounts of his day-to-day survival, ethical dilemmas as an anthropologist, and personal involvement with the Sirionó provided some of the background information I had been seeking. I read of Holmberg's constant battles with infections, dysentery, heat, humidity, and insects. For the first time I began to comprehend his problem of acclimating to the lowland environment after spending his life in cold climates. It was also evident from the journals that his bouts of illness were compounded by the emotional stress of his field experience in Casarabe, the site in eastern Bolivia selected for his research.

Casarabe was a Sirionó "Indian School" operated by the Bolivian military. The encampment, about 60 kilometers southeast of Trinidad, capital of Beni province, had been visited briefly by explorer-ethnographer Alfred Métraux. As a visitor to the Yale campus, Métraux had encouraged the young graduate student to pursue his dissertation research among this little-known group.

In 1940, Holmberg flew to La Paz, where he obtained permission from the government to live and work in Casarabe. He then flew to Trinidad, in those days truly a last outpost of civilization. Mounted on a riding ox, he made the two-day trip through mud, swamps, forest and plains to Casarabe. There the army built him a small house and he settled into camp routine.

As I read further, Holmberg's disillusionment with conditions at Casarabe became more and more apparent. He was appalled at the treatment of the Indians, who were expected to work long hours in the fields and were frequently beaten if they refused. Holmberg was in an untenable position. He could do little to alleviate the suffering of the Sirionó because he was a guest of the Bolivian government in their encampment and would have been expelled for his efforts. He became increasingly marginalized. The Indians didn't trust him because he was associated, though tenuously, with the army officers running the "school." He began to stay away from the Bolivians, both to assuage his own conscience and to attempt to gain better rapport with the Sirionó. During most of his stay at Casarabe, Holmberg feigned an imperfect knowledge of Spanish to avoid continuous contact with camp personnel. To make matters worse, he had come to Bolivia to study what he had been led to believe were *unacculturated* Sirionó only to be trapped in a situation of forced acculturation under brutal circumstances. His despair was acute. Then, after more than six months of a nightmarish existence, Holmberg was rescued from Casarabe.

Late one afternoon, the "Indian hunter" Luís Silva Sánchez rode into camp. Silva was an expert woodsman, spoke fluent Sirionó and was well known for his success at peacefully contacting unacculturated Sirionó bands. Silva agreed to take Holmberg with him when he returned to Tibaera, an Indian Camp Silva had established on the Río Blanco. Luís Silva also worked the settlement with Sirionó labor but either did not mistreat the Indians or, more likely, did not do so in Holmberg's presence. Eventually, with Silva's help, Holmberg contacted an unacculturated band of Sirionó and was able to spend several days among them before a serious eye infection forced a retreat to the nearest settlement at Yaguarú.

While Holmberg was with Silva at Tibaera, he carried out his "Adventures in Culture Change," which introduced the Indians to modern agricultural techniques. The results were not particularly encouraging, however, since the Sirionó remained in peonage despite Holmberg's efforts to improve their way of life. Holmberg must have known that as soon as he left Tibaera, the Sirionó would lose the special status his presence had conferred on them. As a graduate student, Holmberg's primary responsibility was to complete his research as proposed—to present his doctoral committee with a study of the hunger drive among unacculturated Sirionó. Although he tried in a limited way, Holmberg had neither the time nor the resources to change the course of events affecting the Sirionó. But he did not forget their situation. Later he would have another chance to help oppressed Indians, during the Vicos project in Peru.

In addition to providing background information and insights into Sirionó acculturation during those early years, Holmberg's journal pinpointed areas of Sirionó habitation. My next task, one that could be carried out only in Bolivia would be to determine where the Sirionó were at present and if they were still a viable society. I also had to consider the disquieting possibility that there were no longer any Sirionó left to study.

During the summer of 1982, I returned to Bolivia to begin my search for the Sirionó and additional knowledge of their past. This quest led me into a series of unexpected encounters with people in some of the most remote areas of the lowlands. As John Steinbeck related in *Travels with Charley*:

> Once a journey is designed, equipped, and put in process a new factor enters and takes over. A trip, a safari, an exploration, is an entity, different from all other journeys. It has personality, temperament, individuality, uniqueness. A journey is a person in itself; no two are alike. And all plans, safeguards, policing, and coercion are fruitless. We find after years of struggle that we do not take a trip; a trip takes us.

Since my point of entry was Santa Cruz, I began in those areas of Sirionó territory accessible from the Santa Cruz region: the Franciscan missions of the Apostolic Vicariate of Ñúflo de Chávez, established as *reducciones* for the Guarayo Indians but also including the southernmost range of the Sirionó. Salvatierra, where the curious photos of nude Sirionó had been taken, was one of these missions. Since I had no idea where Salvatierra was located in the Vicariate, I needed to do some groundwork in Santa Cruz. A close friend and an American Catholic missionary, Ray Cowell, volunteered that the Franciscan Center House was there in the city and that the superior no doubt could help. At the Center on the outskirts of Santa Cruz, the superior showed me maps of the region and gave me names of Franciscan nuns and priests who would be able to assist me. When I questioned him about the history of the mission, he explained that he knew only generalities but that the man who built the mission was there. I was warned, however, that Salvatierra's founder, Hildebert Wolpert, was very old and quite senile. Father Wolpert was summoned. He was a small, spry man with a shock of white hair and very blue eyes. I spoke to him in Spanish, but he answered in German. The superior apologetically smiled and said Father Wolpert did not seem to know where he was. I experienced a terrible sense of loss. Here was a man who had a lifetime of incredible experiences locked forever in his aging mind. I repeated a few pleasantries, and Father Wolpert retired to the garden to sit in the shade, staring vacantly at the sky. I took solace in having seen and met the man who founded Salvatierra and in having made some link, however small, with the Sirionó past I was trying to uncover.

My journey to Salvatierra had unauspicious beginnings. The bus service to Asención de Guarayos, the capital of the Vicariate and my jumping-off place, had been interrupted indefinitely. The unpaved section of the road from the Okinawa agricultural colony to the Río Grande was almost impassable because of recent heavy rains. Undaunted, I set out anyway, getting as far as Okinawa, a mere 80 kilometers down the road—only 300 to go. I stood at the end of the pavement, contemplating the 15 kilometers of mud ahead. It began to drizzle, and my resolve to reach Salvatierra at all costs began to falter. Then a jeep came along; it passed through the Okinawa settlement, obviously making a try for the river. I flagged it down, and the two men inside, geologists on their way to San Ramón, agreed to take me that far, assuming we could make it through the quagmire.

The 15 kilometers took four hours. We got badly mired twice, but successfully dug out, finally reaching the river. By now the drizzle was a steady rain and it was getting colder as the souther, or *surazo*, moved across the land. We were chilled and miserable from repeated bouts with knee-high mud and the sticky slop thrown up by the wheels of the jeep as we dug and pushed our way along.

CHAPTER ONE

Crossing the river on a big flat-bottomed barge proved uneventful, as was the 70-kilometer trip up a graveled road to San Ramón. On the way, with the heat turned up and packed in among the supplies, we watched our clothes steam and the mud on them crust over. Although I was stiff, cramped, and filthy, it felt marvelous to be warm. All too soon we reached San Ramón, where the geologists abandoned me to the elements and went on their way. It was getting dark, so after a few inquiries I found a small hotel on the Ascención road and checked in. All I wanted was a shower and bed—food could wait. No sooner had I filled out my registration form than a pickup truck stopped in front of the hotel and the driver announced he was on his way to Ascención. I knew it might be days before another chance would come along so, after talking to the driver, I climbed in the back of the truck with six other people. The trip to Ascención seemed interminable. It got darker and colder. We all huddled close to the cab to get out of the wind, but soon even that didn't help. We arrived in Ascención around 9 p.m. I was let off in front of the Franciscan convent but was so numb with cold I could barely make it through the gates to ring the bell. When the door finally opened, I was shivering violently. A nun in a spotless gray and white habit stared at me. I suppose she was trying to determine whether I was male or female and how to deal with this muddy, mute apparition in her doorway. Finally, I removed my stocking hat and spoke to her. Convinced that I was indeed a woman, the nun brought me inside and began pouring down hot tea. I was fed, directed to a guest house, and left alone. No one asked who I was or why I was there. The shower was cold but the bed was soft and had two heavy wool blankets. I was asleep instantly.

Early the next morning, I was awakened by the same nun who had met me at the door. She told me breakfast would be ready at the main house in fifteen minutes. Seated at a long table and surrounded by gray and white habits I was questioned by the nun at the head of the table. I explained to her that I was trying to get to Urubichá where, the Franciscan superior in Santa Cruz had told me, a Sister Ludmilla would assist me in getting to Salvatierra. One of the nuns suggested I talk to Father Aurelio who would be going to Urubichá that same day to say Mass.

Father Aurelio was willing to take me along but explained that he would be going to Yaguarú first to visit a very old nun who had been in the mission field for over fifty years. I remembered Holmberg having mentioned the village of Yaguarú and explained to the priest that it would certainly not be out of my way and no doubt would be interesting. Father Aurelio had a new four-wheel-drive truck that made the trip easily and we arrived well before lunch. He showed me the town, little more than an old adobe church and a few houses clustered around an open plaza in which horses and cows were grazing.

The old nun had lunch waiting for us when we returned from our tour. Like all of the Franciscans I had met thus far, she was Austrian and, in spite of so many years in Bolivia, spoke Spanish with a very heavy accent. She explained that she was a nurse and operated the small clinic in Yaguarú. Then I remembered that this was where Luís Silva had brought Holmberg, almost blind from an eye infection contracted in the forest while they were traveling with some Sirionó. Never expecting that this woman would have witnessed or even remembered an event that occurred over forty years ago, I nonetheless asked if she recalled a young, blonde American who came there in 1941. She searched her memory, smiled and said, "Yes, I do remember. He was very thin and exhausted. A Bolivian man led him by the hand to my clinic. The young man had a terrible eye infection. That was before we had antibiotics, you know, but I had sulfa and treated him with that. He was here for two weeks. I remember that he gave his Bolivian friend some of his money and asked him to use it to buy food for himself and the Indians. There were some Indians with them, and they camped on the edge of town until the young man's eyes were better. Then he went off with them." Again, I experienced that same sense of wonderment at having touched the past that I felt when in the presence of Father Hildebert. But, like the old priest, the nun's advanced age prevented her from dredging up any additional knowledge of Holmberg or the Sirionó. Still, I was grateful for the chance quirk of fate that brought me to Yaguarú to meet her.

Later that afternoon, Father Aurelio and I drove to Urubichá where I was introduced to Sister Ludmilla and a young nursing nun, Sister Walena. Sister Walena told me she would be going to Salvatierra, a 20-kilometer trip by horse, in a day or two. She added that she tried to make the trip twice a month to treat the sick there.

After two days at the convent in Urubichá I was eager to get to Salvatierra. In my youth I had found nuns to be mysterious and intriguing creatures and had romanticized about life in a convent. My last two days rapidly dispelled any aspirations I may have had for a monastic existence. Ludmilla ran a very tight ship.

Once Walena and I left Urubichá, the young nun seemed to relax and began to smile and talk animatedly. She rode well, which challenged some of my stereotypes, although there was something incongruous about a nun in full habit sitting astride a horse. It was a long trip, particularly since we had to cross three deep rivers which involved unsaddling the horses, canoeing ourselves and the tack across, returning to tow the horses behind the canoe on long tethers, and then saddling up again.

We reached Salvatierra at sunset. It stood on a high bank across the last river we would have to ford. It was a beautiful, truly mesmerizing sight. The miniature whitewashed church and bell tower stood on a small knoll surrounded by orange and grapefruit trees laden with fruit. The setting sun gave everything a rosy hue that seemed unreal. But my euphoria was short lived: Salvatierra turned out to be one of the most depressing places I have ever been.

"Salvatierra"

TWO
Chapter 2

Walena and I stayed at the mission compound, which since Father Hildebert's retirement, was virtually abandoned. An older Guarayo woman named Concepción, shortened to "Concha," was watching over the place. That first night, Concha silently served us some hot tea and bread we had brought along for the trip and then disappeared into the kitchen. I slept in what had been Franciscan Brother Yocundo's room; Walena took the room next door, Father Hildebert's old quarters. Everything was dirty and in disrepair. The bats screeched around up under the roof tiles for most of the night, and everytime I shined my flashlight on a wall half a dozen large roaches scurried for cover.

The next morning Walena made her rounds. I volunteered to come along since I thought this would be a good opportunity to begin meeting some of the people. In the glare of the morning sun, the village lost some of its charm. Everything had an air of decay. The houses were laid out along straight, long streets, which were littered with refuse. Each house was a "duplex", — two large rooms separated by a center wall with one family in each room. The houses were plastered adobe brick with tile roofs, a reflection of the efforts of the once-resident priest. Most villages outside the mission area were simple wattle-and-daub with thatched roofs. Although it was evident that these had been well-built homes, some now had walls in partial collapse, others were missing tiles, and some no longer had doors (all made in the mission carpentry).

Since the Indians traditionally sleep in hammocks, there was a large center post in every room to which one end of each hammock was tied. The other end was tied to one of the several posts set into the dirt floor near an outside wall. Thus, when all the hammocks were hung, the center post resembled a Maypole. Walena and I went from room to room visiting the sick. With the exception of one old woman who had a dislocated shoulder, everyone we examined was suffering from some respiratory illness. In each house, we found two or three people lying listlessly in their hammocks. Many of the ill were older people, and Walena explained that a high percentage of these were the "original" inhabitants, the Sirionó brought to the mission by Father Hildebert years ago. Most of the sick were running high fevers and were racked by spasms of coughing, spitting up blood-flecked sputum. We administered antibiotics and medicines for fever and coughing. The people seemed grateful for both the medicine and the attention.

Walena told me that many of the older Indians had tuberculosis, which I had suspected, and that alcohol abuse had made them difficult to treat. She gave them vitamins and other remedies but felt that they were slowly dying in spite of her efforts. Some of the younger people were following the same pattern.

Not eager to spend another night in Salvatierra, Walena was ready to return to Urubichá by late afternoon. She presented me with an assortment of pills and syrups and a list of patients and their doses. When she saw me hesitate to take them, she said that it was difficult to leave these things with the people since they often did not understand how much they should take. Reluctantly, I agreed to pass out medicine three times a day for the next fourteen days. Walena then rode off into the sunset, leaving me with the assurance that she would be back for me in two weeks.

I woke up the next morning with a sore throat and fever. It had also turned rainy and cold again, which contributed to my sense of gloom. The first day of my illness I lay in the hammock in my room feeling sorry for myself and generally wretched. I made the rounds visiting my "patients" but was in no mood to chat or offer any words of encouragement. The second day, the steady drizzle continued, and, typically, it was much colder. My room was dark, cold, and depressing. I moved into the kitchen to sit by the warmth of the fire and over the next three days, Concha and I got to know one another.

Although she had no idea of her age, Concha must have been about fifty-eight, judging by events she mentioned. At first, she was just someone to talk to, to help pass the long hours as I sat huddled by the fire. As the stories poured out, with little urging on my part, I realized I had happened on an extraordinary informant. I got out my notebook and began writing things down. Rather than inhibit Concha, my recording of her recollections seemed to make her even more eager to talk. In the midst of all this talk,

Cocha remarked what a strange coincidence it was that we should meet in Salvatierra or that we should have even met at all. Normally, she said, she lived alone in a small house about a kilometer from Urubichá. Only a week before I arrived, Sister Ludmilla had asked her to go to Salvatierra to look after the mission while the regular caretaker was in the Urubichá clinic giving birth. Concha then continued with her storytelling, mentioning in passing the name Luís Silva. I sat upright in my chair.

"Luís Silva Sánchez?"

"The same."

"You actually knew him?"

Concha laughed. "Knew him? I *know* him! His son is married to my daughter."

All I could do was stare at her. I had been certain that Silva must be dead by now. For this reason, I hadn't seriously considered trying to locate him, a task which could have taken weeks or even months. Now, as the result of an improbable coincidence, I had met one of the few people in the region who knew the whereabouts of Holmberg's old friend and guide. All that, however, would come later. In the meantime, there was Salvatierra.

Concha's stories of her life were intertwined with those of the Sirionó. During the 1930s, the Sirionó began to appear regularly at mestizo homesteads, usually to steal crops and farm animals. From time to time a farmer would be wounded or killed during these raids. The Sirionó were being pursued by an Indian group from the south whom they called the Yanaiguas but who are known more generally as the Ayoreos. The Ayoreos had entered Sirionó territory, killing men and taking women and children as slaves. No longer safe in the forest, the Sirionó began moving closer to mestizo settlements where the Ayoreos were unlikely to follow. Restricted in their movements, the Sirionó could not feed themselves and were forced to engage in raiding. Some even sought the protection of ranchers in the Guarayos region, suddenly appearing at the fringes of the forest, hands held out empty as a sign of peace. Because of increased raiding, the local ranchers with the help of the military began hunting the Sirionó either to capture or to exterminate them. Recognizing this threat, Concha explained, several of the Franciscan priests decided to set up missions specifically for Sirionó. Salvatierra was one of these. To gather up the forest Indians, Father Hildebert and Brother Yocundo relied on the assistance of a Sirionó headman, or *ererecua*, who had come out with his band at the Santa María mission southwest of Salvatierra. This man was Samboó.

The Franciscans rarely accompanied Samboó and his few selected companions on these expeditions to contact unacculturated Sirionó. The group would be outfitted for the trip with steel tools, clothing, and staples such as rice and bananas. Invariably, they would find a small band of forest

Sirionó, oftentimes half-starved from having just fled an Ayoreo or mestizo attack. With gifts of food, tools, and shirts, Samboó quickly gained their confidence, and after a few days they would be willing to return with him to Salvatierra. The initial "capture" was relatively easy. Keeping the Sirionó at Salvatierra, however, was another thing.

Public whippings were common at Indian missions. But then all farm laborers, mestizo and Indian alike, were customarily whipped with a rawhide *huasca* when they failed to perform given tasks. These whippings were seldom administered by the priests, but by Indian leaders or *caciques*. The caciques frequently were men who had been selected to perform leadership roles by the priests and not necessarily by their own people. They, too, would be subject to sanctions if they failed to meet work schedules or exercise control over the labor force. Although mission Indians did not labor for the profit of a *patrón* as did those on farms and ranches, they were still required to be in the fields six days a week from dawn until dark. Work in and of itself was seen by Europeans, whether religious or secular, as a major "civilizing" force. Thus, missionaries like Father Hildebert required their Indian charges to work three days a week on their own family parcels and the remaining three days for the mission. In addition, a cattle herd was gradually built up to supply meat, milk, and cheese for the mission. This herd was worked by Indian *vaqueros* (cowboys) but strictly overseen by the priest, who was constantly on guard against pilferage. Since cows were slaughtered only on special feast days such as Christmas, New Year's, and Easter, the Indians had to depend on game for the remainder of their meat supply. As the result of almost continual hunting, the area around the mission was rapidly depleted of wildlife. Consequently, the temptation presented by cattle roaming alone in the woods was too great to withstand. The killing and eating of mission cattle was a crime punishable by a severe beating, the withholding of rations, and an additional work load.

The Guarayo Indians, already sedentary farmers at the time of European contact and accustomed to paying labor taxes to their caciques, adapted well to mission life. They were permitted to continue brewing corn beer, and a certain amount of merrymaking and drunkenness was allowed on feast days. Except for the addition of a thin veneer of Christianity, their lives probably did not change dramatically. For the Sirionó, however, mission life was intolerable. Not accustomed to the rigors of working in the hot sun hour after hour, they were beaten continually for escaping to a nearby spot of shade to rest and talk. They were also very good at hunting and consuming mission cattle, a serious whipping offense. When Sirionó patience ran out, the ererecua would take his band back into the forest, carrying along a few tools and pieces of clothing.

It seemed that no sooner had Father Hildebert settled one group of

Sirionó at Salvatierra than another would take off into the woods. Samboó was kept busy chasing down the runaways, giving them gifts and encouraging them to return to the mission. After several years of this, a new tactic was tried.

Concha was a young girl the day Father Hildebert rode into Urubichá and announced he was looking for Guarayo men and women to marry with the "Chori," the local term used for the Sirionó. It means "savages" and Concha used it interchangeably with *bárbaro*, the Spanish term for the uncivilized. Throughout my travels, I found that "Chori" was the locally accepted label for the Sirionó but one which the Indians considered derogatory. I asked Concha why the Guarayos were willing to marry Sirionó if they considered them to be inferior.

Concha explained that Urubichá, like many Guarayo villages, had a small, closely related population which made it difficult to find a suitable spouse. Besides, she laughed, the Sirionó men were tall, handsome and fierce-looking, evidently an irresistible combination for Guarayo women. The Guarayo men also found Sirionó women to their liking, and Father Hildebert's plan worked. Young Sirionó men and women were paired with Guarayos. Once this occurred the solidarity of the band was broken, the ererecua lost his power, and the Sirionó for the most part stayed put. This experiment was carried out at other missions in the Guarayo region, resulting in the gradual assimilation of the Sirionó into Guarayo culture.

During these early years at Salvatierra, many of the Sirionó contracted smallpox and influenza, which decimated their numbers. Concha, who visited the mission frequently to stay with relatives, remembered those times when ten or fifteen Sirionó would die in the span of a few days. In those years, she related, there was little that could be done for them. One afternoon, Concha took me up to the small hill overlooking the village where the cemetery was located. Spreading her arms, she indicated where the early inhabitants had been buried. A few wooden crosses stood here and there, probably from more recent burials. The remainder of the area was grass and scrub, with only the unevenness of the ground to mark the nature of its use. "Many, many died," Concha said, almost in a whisper. "I have never seen such fevers, they burned up from the fire in their bodies."

When Concha married, she and her husband left the Guarayo area for regions to the north. They were *enpatronado*, taken on by a rancher from the Beni who, in exchange for a little money, alcohol, and promises of more, indentured them for five years. After her second child was born, Concha's husband left her for another woman. Concha then began living with Isaías Suárez, a rancher who, finding her attractive, paid the debt she had incurred with her first patrón so she could accompany him to his settlement on the Río Blanco. This seems to have occurred about 1945. Shortly after Concha's arrival at the Suárez homestead, she met Isaías' best friend, Luís Silva. Silva had abandoned Tibaera, clearing a new farmstead upriver, Las Piedras, but made frequent trips by canoe to visit his friend. Concha said they were both prodigious drinkers, often spending weeks together when they were seldom sober. Both Suárez and Silva had Sirionó working on their farms and because the Sirionó and Guarayo languages are both of Guaraní origin, Concha learned to speak Sirionó quickly. She spent a great deal of time with the women, instructing them in female chores and often sharing one of their clay pipes late in the evening when the work was done. Concha felt sorry for the Sirionó. Their life was in the forest, not in the fields. They were never so happy as when they were off hunting or talking about a hunt. The Sirionó, like others in peonage, were whipped if they did not work. But, Concha said, they could not stand up to the whippings like the rest of the peons. For everyone else it was the way of life, but the Sirionó were shamed and humiliated each time it happened. Just as at Salvatierra, many would escape into the wilderness. Invariably, they would be found and brought back or would appear on someone else's land, looking for food, clothing, and tools.

At this time, Concha related, there were Sirionó on farms and ranches all along the Río Blanco and nearby areas. Some had been taken as children when the mestizos would come across a band of Sirionó in the wilderness. When the Indians scattered, the slower moving children frequently were taken captive. They would be brought up as servants, *criados*, always treated as "Chori" but knowing little about their Indian origins. I later met several of these individuals who lived out their lives in isolation, rejected by their adopted mestizo culture but not wanting to have anything to do with their Sirionó counterparts.

Also during these early years, the Sirionó spent a great deal of time floating from farm to farm, from mission to mission. Certain groups and their leaders became well known throughout the region. They would appear at a Guarayo mission, accept gifts, stay and work for a while, and then disappear back into the woods. Several weeks or months later they would emerge somewhere else to repeat the process. As more Sirionó married non-Sirionó and even greater numbers were killed or succumbed to illness, the Sirionó gradually stabilized on missions and farms throughout what had been their old hunting territory. By the mid-1950s, Concha no longer saw or heard of new Sirionó bands appearing out of the forest.

Concha and I sat out the remainder of the bad weather in the warmth of the kitchen while my cold slowly improved. I continued making house calls and was becoming better acquainted with many of the residents of Salvatierra. During the cold spell, most people remained inside their houses. Doors and windows were closed against the wind while people lay in their hammocks covered with a thin blanket or flour sack sheet. Underneath each hammock a small fire was kept burning day and night. As I entered a house from the cold and drizzle outside, I was enveloped by a warm, smoky darkness. The small fires gave just enough light to see by as I moved from hammock to hammock visiting the sick. The heavy smoke made the large, dank, living areas comfortably warm, but soon my eyes would be running and my throat burning. Those people with respiratory illness no doubt were made worse by the smoke, coughing and spitting almost constantly but the alternative was the bone-chilling cold.

When the sun finally broke through the clouds after five days of wind, rain, and cold, people began to emerge from their houses and the town once again appeared populated. With the warming trend, the house fires were extinguished and there was a remarkable improvement in many of those I had been treating. Daily activities which had virtually halted during the surazo were resumed.

The women's activities centered around two primary tasks: weaving hammocks and making chicha. The Guarayos, like the Sirionó and many other lowland South American Indians, had made string hammocks in aboriginal times. This was a relatively uncomplicated process involving the twining of string from bark or tree cotton and then wrapping the string around two posts set apart about a body-length. Once the posts had been wrapped, the number of turns determining the width of the hammock, several cross strings would be tied to hold the twine in place. Then, the looped ends would be carefully removed from the posts and a rope passed through the loops to secure them, and the hammock was ready for use. With the arrival of the Franciscans, the Guarayo women were taught to weave on a primitive, upright loom which could be made from local materials. Tree cotton and, later, imported threads were used in this process along with European dyes to create an imaginative, colorful product. The Guarayo hammock may take well over two months to complete, but the financial return is considered worth the effort: Some hammocks bring as much as U.S. $50.00, a substantial amount of money in a village like Salvatierra.

Between periods at the loom, the women are busy with the preparation of chicha, a mildly alcoholic beer made from corn or manioc. As I discovered, however, the consumption of chicha does not occur solely as a social event. When it is available, which is almost always, chicha is drunk continuously by every member of the family. Because the preparation of chicha is so time-consuming and the resulting beverage has the advantage of being storable, it is extremely important in the diet of the Guarayo. Some people, I observed, would go several days consuming little else but chicha. An adult man or woman can eaily down two liters of the home brew in just one visit to the family crock.

Guarayo chicha is prepared by first boiling corn or manioc until it is soft. This mash is then formed into cakes or patties which are placed in a wooden platter. Next women, children, or anyone else available sit around the platter and chew on the cakes which, after mastication, are spat into a container. Mixed with saliva, the mash begins to ferment. The fermentation takes two to three days, or longer if a more potent beer is desired. It is then boiled again and placed in pottery crocks buried to the neck in the floor of the house. The burial keeps the chicha pleasantly cool and protects the crock from breakage. Placed over the opening is a large gourd which serves both as a lid and a drinking cup.

Although the Sirionó had made mead from honey and sweet potatoes, manioc, or corn, this custom no longer exists in Salvatierra. Curiously, the remaining older Sirionó in the village apparently have not substituted Guarayo chicha for mead. While those living with Guarayos consume chicha, I did not see any of the older Sirionó actively involved in the almost continuous production of the beverage. On the other hand, they, like the Guarayos, will go to almost any length to obtain cane alcohol. Concha told me that while Fr. Hildebert was living in Salvatierra, he controlled the presence of alcohol in the village. He could not, however, prevent people from going elsewhere to drink. Still, while the old priest was present, drunkness among the residents was only occasional. He did not interfere with the making of chicha, no doubt well aware that it formed an important part of the diet, and, according to Concha, he enjoyed drinking it with the Indians. When well-aged chicha is consumed a mild inebriation results, but many of the villagers I talked to agreed that it doesn't "make you crazy" like the 96-proof alcohol distilled in the sugar mills.

Although the price for a 25-liter can of cane alcohol may vary according to the current value of the peso, it always presents a substantial expenditure of money. A full can (cheaper than buying it in Urubichá by the bottle) must be brought 60 kilometers, often backpacked the entire distance, from Ascención where is it sold. Once the owner of the can arrives in Salvatierra, he or she will save a few liters for personal consumption and sell off the remainder to villagers with cash to pay for it, thus sharing with others the cost of the 25 liters. It is also common for several people to pool their resources for a can or even two. Fights may result if the participants in this venture feel they haven't gotten their fair share.

Obtaining money to buy alcohol causes strife in the community, particularly among spouses. Women will participate in the buying, selling, and consumption of alcohol; but there is much greater criticism of women who drink to excess than of men, so it is women who most frequently object to the expenditure of family resources for this purpose. As in most small, remote villages like Salvatierra, cash is hard to come by. Women often have larger cash reserves as a result of their hammock making. The men occasionally shoot wild game such as peccaries, curing the hide and drying and salting the meat and taking the skins and meat to Urubichá to be sold. Crops also may bring in some seasonal income, but most villagers plant only small plots: about one hectare of rice mixed with corn and another area of manioc, plantains, and bananas usually planted in the previous year's clearing. The only other way for men to earn income is to leave Salvatierra and hire out on nearby farms and ranches as laborers. Even then, much of the money earned goes for living expenses and alcohol and very little is brought back to the village. As a result, men must often go to their wives when they want drinking money. If the woman is not agreeable to giving up her own savings, a verbal barrage ensues which may escalate into physical violence. If the man is already drunk when he demands more money, the situation can become critical. Women and children have been wounded with shotguns when an enraged husband or father grabbed his weapon and fired blindly. On two occasions, frightened women came running with their husbands' guns to beg Concha to hide the weapons somewhere in the church compound. During my stay in the village, the drinking bouts never ceased, and at two or three houses there was always a disturbance. Those not participating would be angry at having their sleep interrupted and would join in the shouting but would be just as likely to cause the same problem a few days later. I asked Concha if it was always like this in Salvatierra or had I arrived during a period when drinking was more prevalent? She responded in disgust that the people of Salvatierra were real "chupacos" (drunkards).

My purpose in coming to Salvatierra was to ascertain the current situation of the Sirionó there and to assess its feasibility as a future research site. It took only a few days to determine that very little remained of the Sirionó or their culture, and I was faced with the possibility that Salvatierra and places like it were all that was left of these people. No doubt this thought and the combination of bad weather, sickness in the village, pervasive drunkenness and violence, and my own illness contributed to my feelings of futility and depression. For a time, I considered leaving early, walking by myself back to Urubichá. I could easily justify this decision on the grounds that I had other sites to visit and could make more profitable use of my time elsewhere. Deep inside, however, I knew I was quitting, fleeing from Salvatierra and what it represented. If I left, who could I entrust with the responsibility of handing out medication—the responsibility I had agreed to accept? I gritted my teeth and decided to make the best of it. Since I was stuck in Salvatierra for at least another week before Sr. Walena was due to arrive, I could spend some time finding out more about the town and its residents. Concha, away from home and just as bored and fed up with Salvatierra as I was, became an eager field assistant. During the next week, we mapped the town (Fig. 1), counted the inhabitants (142), and visited the

Figure 1

SALVATIERRA

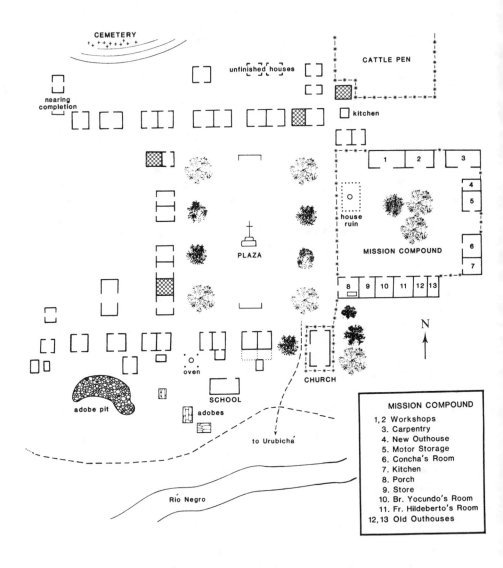

older Sirionó. In retrospect my remaining there was a good decision. Albeit not enthusiastically, I gathered bits and pieces of information which later gave me a breadth of understanding I would not otherwise have had.

Concha and I first determined that of the several hundred Sirionó brought to Salvatierra during the 1930s and 1940s, only eleven of the original inhabitants remained (Fig. 2). The rest had died or moved elsewhere. The children and grandchildren of the eleven survivors were culturally, if not biologically, Guarayo. As a result, most of what was Sirionó culture was forgotten, hidden, or repressed. Alone in their houses, the few older Sirionó would converse in their own language; but when others entered, Sirionó would be dropped for Guarayo. Some of the men still saved beeswax and feathers to make arrows, but these materials were generally stored out of sight. Concha was of inestimable value when I tried to question the older Sirionó about their past. Because Concha spoke their language fluently, the Indians were more at ease with her; and once they perceived that I was not there to criticize or make fun of them, the talk came more freely. Together, we would visit some of the older people, and, while Concha translated from Sirionó to Spanish, I would listen to tales like the following told by Marcos Maire:

"I was about eight years old when we were brought out of the forest the first time. I remember that our houses there were just piled-up palm leaves. I remember once we came across an old mestizo man who was alone fishing at a lake; he was killed for his machete and clothes. We wanted clothes because they kept us warm and the insects could not bite us. We also killed

Figure 2. Remaining "Original" Sirionó in Salvatierra

(Rosendo) Eoco
(Nicolás) Eronde
(Francisco) Curucua
(Marcos) Maire
(Magdalena) Barae (wife of Maire)
*(José) Erameya
*(Candelaria) Eretsa Ea (wife of Erameya)
(Nicolás) Nambu
(Norotea) Ea (wife of Nambu)
»(Esteban) Chonti
»(Asunta) Arirenque (wife of Chonti)

*Erameya and Chonti are siblings as are Eretsa Ea and Arirenque. Marriage was brother-sister exchange.

21

the mestizos for axes and machetes. Then the ererecua Samboó came with his men and brought us gifts. At first, we did not want to go with him, but he gave us rice and axes so we came. Samboó took us to Padre Francisco's mission at Santa María but many went back into the forest because of too much work. Then Samboó brought them back again. Almost all are dead now. Then Padre Hildeberto came and brought us here to Salvatierra where he and Hermano Yocundo were building a town. My wife, Barae, was also at Santa María. She had already borne one child when I met her [Marco's way of explaining that Barae was several years older than he]. Padre Hildeberto married us here in Salvatierra. We have only one daughter. Five of our children died while still in their mother's arms."

After Marcos had finished his story, I noticed a couple of arrows standing behind some clothing hanging on the wall. Marcos followed my gaze, got up from the mat on the floor where he had been sitting, and brought the arrows over to me. I examined them with great care, trying perhaps too hard to convey my appreciation for his handwork. "Would you like to buy them?" I was taken aback. How could he offer to a stranger something he had spent days making and had obviously kept for some time? Then I realized it was I, not Marcos, who valued his arrows. To him, they were just arrows; and as he explained, he had sold quite a few to interested visitors like me over the past several decades. Although certainly not a frequent source of income, Sirionó men like Marcos always kept a bow and a few arrows around just in case one of Salvatierra's infrequent visitors would like to buy these now hard-to-come-by artifacts. Selling bows and arrows was one more way of earning cash. I was a little uneasy about buying Marcos' arrows because the price he asked was ridiculously low for something which in another few years would no longer exist. But I agreed, and after dark when few of the townspeople would see him, Marcos brought a bow and two arrows over to the priest's house.

The following day, Concha and I returned to Marcos' and Barae's house but it was closed up tight. There was no padlock on the door so it had been locked from the inside. I looked at Concha in puzzlement. Concha put her ear against the door.

"They're in there," she said. Then she spoke a few words of Sirionó through the crack in the door. There was a muffled response.

"They're drinking." Concha shrugged her shoulders and started back toward the church. I caught up with her.

"But why are they all locked up?" I asked.

"So they won't have to share with anyone," she replied.

For three days and nights Marcos and Barae stayed inside their shuttered house. I was despondent. It was my money that had instigated yet another drinking bout. Concha was noncommittal. Then she told me about the man who came to the village a few years ago to photograph the Indians. He brought alcohol and money for them so they would go with him into the forest and remove their clothes to be photographed. Everyone thought it was a big joke. Besides, they got good money and two cans of alcohol for their efforts. I had found the answer to the mystery of the photos of nude Sirionó men. But it made me heartsick to realize that I was being lumped with those who had come to exploit the Indians.

Time passed slowly in spite of my efforts to fill the hours with useful work, and I still had two or three days left in Salvatierra. I had been spending part of my time helping Concha feed us, sharing in the cooking chores and pounding corn into meal so we could make chicha and some hard, baked corn cakes called _biscochos_. Even though I had money to pay for it, we rarely ate meat. Most of the meat brought in from hunts was dried and taken to Urubichá where it had been "spoken for" earlier. A few staples such as sugar or salt would be brought back, but more frequently it was alcohol. Concha and I subsisted for days at a time, like everyone else, on chicha, roasted plantains, and boiled manioc. I became obsessed with meat, thinking and talking about it constantly. Concha's grandson (who was staying with her) now and then would bring home a fish from the river and we would cook it whole over the fire. My jaws ached as the steam and fish odor filled the kitchen, and I would entertain such unworthy thoughts as what it would be like not to have to share it.

The day finally arrived when Sr. Walena and the horses appeared on the other side of the river. Concha and I parted fondly. She had another two or three weeks left before she would be relieved of her caretaking duties. I had been a source of entertainment and distraction for her, and I knew she dreaded the solitary days ahead. Like Orpheus, I fought looking back over my shoulder as we rode away from the river toward Urubichá. But I did, and the memory of Salvatierra shall forever haunt me.

"Barae"

the "ARABA"

Searman '84

THREE
Chapter 3

When we arrived in Urubichá, I asked Sr. Ludmilla for assistance in getting to Silva's homestead, Las Piedras, on the Río Blanco. Since the river passed near Urubichá, it was a matter of hiring someone to take me downriver. Concha had told me it was about a five-day trip. But try as we might, we couldn't find anyone with a boat and a working outboard motor. Reluctantly, I gave it up and went back to Ascención with Fr. Aurelio. Fortunately, the bus was running again, so early the following morning I was on my way back to Santa Cruz. The weather had turned hot once more, the road was dry,and we moved along quickly in spite of frequent stops to pick up passengers and their cargoes. By the time we reached the Río Grande, we looked like a caricature of the proverbial Latin American rural bus: people hanging out of doors and windows, bags, boxes, and stems of green plantains tied to the roof rack, and the inevitable array of pigs, ducks, and chickens.

We were loaded on a large, flat-bottomed barge which was towed across the river, now quite low, by a team of men. As the bus was being offloaded, the front wheels slipped off the ramp into the soft sand of the riverbed. The rear wheels remained hung on the barge's prow. For three hours, men took turns digging and levering until the wheels were freed and stabilized on planks. The driver drove the bus forward and with a thunderous crash, the rear wheels came off the barge and hit the planking. The passengers climbed aboard and once again we were on our way. It was dark by the time we reached Santa Cruz. I had never realized what a welcoming sight the lights of the city could be.

After a few day's rest, I took a commercial jet north to Trinidad, the capital of the Beni province. On the plane, I met an older Beniano who was familiar with the region. I briefly told him about Luís Silva Sánchez and my attempts to get to Las Piedras. The man hadn't heard of either Silva or his homestead but reasoned that if the place were five days from Urubichá, it could be reached more quickly from the Beni end of the Río Blanco. He suggested I fly from Trinidad to El Carmen del Iténez, which was on the weekly military transport flight schedule. From El Carmen, he said, it should be relatively easy to find a canoe going upriver since the northern parts of the Río Blanco were much more heavily populated than the regions near Urubichá. He admonished me, however, that the tickets for the flight could not be purchased more than one day in advance and that there were only twenty spaces available. To make matters worse, the plane made three other stops, so four towns were competing for the seats. The remainder of the plane would be filled with cargo. As soon as I checked into a hotel, I walked to the TAM (Transporte Aéreo Militar) office. It was Monday and the plane was scheduled to leave on Wednesday. I asked what time the office opened on Tuesday and was informed that ticket sales would begin at 7 a.m. The following morning I was sitting there on the doorstep at 5:45 a.m., not only the first person in line but the only person. I was smugly confident.

By 6:15 I was no longer alone. Keeping my place as first in "line" became increasingly difficult as people pushed up against the door on both sides of me. I tried to establish my territorial rights by mentioning that I had been there at 5:45 when it was still dark and the streets were empty, but this tactic was met by cold stares and renewed efforts to move me aside. When the office clerk began to unbolt the door, I realized that if I didn't manage to hold my own, I would be swallowed up in the stampede. I began pushing and shoving back, planting myself firmly in front of the door, asking myself if it was worth all this trouble to find Holmberg's guide.

In the end, I moved faster than everyone else and was the first at the ticket window. "El Carmen, round-trip, one." I shouted somewhat incoherently. Behind the window was an utterly tranquil young woman facing a seething mass of humanity. I marveled at her composure. Then I realized this was probably an almost daily occurrence.

"I can't sell you a round-trip ticket."

"Why not?"

"Because after today's flight, the plane goes into maintenance and we can't guarantee when it will be on line again."

"But why can't you just use another plane?"

She gave me a scathing look. I was beginning to feel like an idiot.

"Because only the 'Araba' can make the landing there."

I didn't dare ask what the "Araba" was. My mind was racing. How could I go to a place knowing there was no way back? In my indecision, the woman behind me saw her chance and began to push in front of me.

In desperation I said, "I'll take the ticket". Once outside, I began to have serious doubts about this latest journey to nowhere.

But the next morning I was packed and at the airport. The flight was scheduled to leave at 6 a.m. but it was almost 10 before we were ushered out onto the tarmac. There it was, the "Araba"—a squat, wide-winged, pot-bellied transport with big, fat tires. The entire aircraft was painted in green and brown camouflage. I was told it was a gift from Israel and no one seemed to know what "Araba" meant.

I do not know what I expected, but I was unprepared to find that the passengers would sit like paratroopers on webbed racks along both sides of the aircraft. The entire center of the cabin was occupied by unsecured cargo: flour and sugar in 100-pound sacks, cartons of soap and sardines, bolts of cloth, and rolls of barbed wire. We had no seat belts, our backs were to the windows and the ceiling-high pile of cargo blocked our view of the passengers across the way. No sooner had we left the ground than people began to throw up. Fortunately, they had brought their own sacks. Since the flight wasn't terribly rough, I began to wonder if it was something cultural.

We made two stops on bumpy, short, unpaved runways, and I quickly developed a healty respect for the Araba's peculiar design. At each stop, cargo and passengers were unloaded and new passengers would board for the return trip to Trinidad. All along the route, people commented on the news that the plane was going into maintenance and it would probably be a month or more until it was back in service. I tried not to think about one remark that it was ten days by horse from El Carmen to Trinidad.

El Carmen del Iténez was no different from many other villages in eastern Bolivia I have lived in and visited over the years. Whitewashed wattle-and-daub houses, some with tile, others with thatched roofs, were clustered around a large open field in which animals grazed. An old adobe church occupied part of one side of the town's unadorned "plaza." Since most villages the size of El Carmen rarely have guest accommodations, my first task was to locate a place to spend the night. I found my way to the *alcalde's*, the mayor's house only to discover that the alcalde was an alcaldesa, a stunning woman in her late forties. Exhibiting the warm hospitality that is the trademark of the Beni, she invited me in for a cold drink and insisted I stay with her. I asked her name, which she said was Neyla Viuda de Richards. Once again, I found myself marveling at the strange hand of fate that had brought me to this particular place. I knew that upriver lay San Pedro, the ranch owned by Frederick Park Richards, an American expatriate who is mentioned in Holmberg's introduction to *Nomads*. Holmberg often visited the Richards' ranch while he was with Silva at Tibaera, enjoying both the hospitality and comradeship offered by the older American. Neyla, of course, was too young to remember Holmberg but said her father-in-law, Frederick, had spoken of him often. Both men must have been very lonely and homesick, she reflected, because before his death Frederick frequently had commented on how he missed having Holmberg around to share stories of the United States with him. I asked Neyla about her involvement with the Richards family and she told me one of those famous stories that seem to abound in the Bolivian lowlands.

Abrahán Richards was Frederick's eldest son. While in his early twenties, he married Neyla's older sister, Angela. According to Neyla, Abrahán was encouraged to marry Angela because of the land and cattle she would bring with her to the marriage. Abrahán's marriage to Angela was not a happy one, and eventually the rancher's eye began to wander. He made frequent trips to El Carmen from San Pedro to visit his wife's younger sister, Neyla. One day, when Angela was absent from the ranch, Abrahán brought Neyla back with him. Hearing what had happened, Angela never returned; to this day, the sisters haven't spoken to one another. Neyla bore Abrahán four sons which brought his progeny to nine. Unfortunately, they did not live happily ever after. For years, Abrahán had been involved in a boundary dispute with another rancher. The boundary post in question had been moved back and forth the disputed two feet for years. One night, after drinking all day with his friends, Abrahán moved the post to within a few feet of the rancher's house. The man swore he would kill him. Knowing Abrahán would be in El Carmen on a particular day, the rancher lay in wait for him beside the road. As Abrahán strode down the road, his enemy stepped out into the sun blocking the path. "I am going to kill you," he told Abrahán while pointing a pistol at him. Abrahán laughed and began to turn aside when the gun was fired. He was struck in the heart and died instantly.

During the retelling of this episode, Neyla showed little emotion. "That's just the way life here is", she said.

"What happened to the man who killed your husband?," I asked.

"He ran away and was gone for a few years. Others took his land and cattle while he was gone so when he came back, there was nothing. He died penniless."

I was given a large, comfortable bed in one of Neyla's four rooms. The roof of the house was thatch and the floor was packed earth, but everything was swept and orderly. In spite of the rustic appearance of the house, the furnishings were quite nice. The front room was occupied by an enormous Sony television set and a Betamax enshrined on a large mahogany table. Promptly at 8 the front room began to fill with people who brought their own chairs. At 8:30 I heard a gasoline generator start up somewhere out near the kitchen. A video cassette was inserted in the Betamax, and we all watched John Wayne in "Río Hondo" in dubbed-in Spanish. No doubt these nightly viewings greatly contributed to Neyla's popularity as the town's mayor.

The following morning I was treated to a Beni ranch breakfast of fried eggs, salad, fresh liver and steak, hot chocolate, and bread. Then Neyla and I began looking for someone to take me to Las Piedras. Just before noon, word came that one of the town's women had hired a canoe to take her upriver to visit a sick relative. Neyla and I walked to the woman's house, and she agreed to take me along. The woman also mentioned that two men who came in on the Araba with me had already spoken to her about the trip, so the canoe would be full. I was a little curious about the men since I hadn't remembered their getting off the plane; but I could have missed them since I had been preoccupied with my own affairs. Later, I asked Neyla if she knew the men and she seemed evasive. I let the matter drop.

We left around three that afternoon with plans to spend the night at San Pedro and then be on our way the next morning. I was excited at the prospect of seeing the Richards ranch although Neyla had told me it was now in the hands of different owners.

The Río Blanco, a curious name for a blackwater river, was glorious. The day was warm, still, and clear. Our motor puttered along, breaking the silence but otherwise undisturbing the scene around us. The river was deep and smooth, with high, steep banks on both sides. Every so often we would pass a small cluster of thatched houses perilously close to the precipice. People would walk to the edge of the riverbank to wave and shout greetings and messages to be carried upriver. The woman who was hosting our trip seemed to know just about everyone.

At dusk we arrived at San Pedro. After reading Holmberg's journal descriptions of his visits to the Richards ranch, I somehow expected an old manor house, an oasis in the wilderness built by an eccentric American living in rustic splendor. To my dismay, the ranch at San Pedro was simply a cluster of thatched houses with a large, tin roofed structure near the river.

The administrator met us at the river's edge and helped unload the canoe. When we reached the large building, there was a small group of people standing around someone sitting in a chair under the roof overhang. I moved closer for a better view. The man in the chair was having teeth pulled by an itinerant dentist. When he left, a woman with a badly swollen jaw sat down and the procedure began again.

I turned away to speak to the administrator about the people at San Pedro. Neyla had told me there were still several families of Sirionó living there, including the old ererecua, Jêjê. The administrator, Antonio, indicated that most of those standing around waiting their turn with the dentist were

"Chori." An older couple was waiting alone near a meat rack so I introduced myself and told them of my quest to locate Sirionó, Luís Silva Sánchez, and any other information about the Sirionó people and their history. The old couple was curious about my trip to the Guarayos region and told me they had relatives there. When I mentioned the people I had met in Salvatierra, they broke into excited Sirionó and called a few more people over. Soon there was a group standing around me asking questions about this person or that one. Some of the names were unfamiliar to me and I had to say so. This brought a moment of silence and then some rapid speculation about whether so-and-so might now be dead. The people told me that Silva was indeed upriver and that he loved to talk about the old days and his "gringo" friend, "Olmber." They had all heard of the young American who had come many years ago to learn their ways and who even went into the forest with Silva to look for the "wild" ones. They also asked me if I had been to Ibiato. I had met with a missionary in Gainesville, Florida, who told me there was a settlement of Sirionó at the old Protestant mission of Ibiato, near Casarabe. At the time, I was surprised to hear this since Holmberg had written, "In 1935 American evangelists founded a mission for the Sirionó at the site of an old Mojo mound called Ibiato, some sixty miles east of Trinidad. By 1940 this mission had a population of about 60 Indians, but could also not be called a successful undertaking."

When I told the Sirionó that I had not yet been to Ibiato but planned on doing so as soon as I returned from this trip, I was again barraged with names of relatives they had there. One man told me he had just returned from Ibiato and that he and his family were considering moving there. The trip had taken a month since they had made the journey on foot. A woman then asked me if I had ever met "Juanito." This was the third time this name had been mentioned during my travels. Concha and Marcos Maire had both talked of the gringo Juanito. Evidently he was a missionary, somehow linked to Ibiato and had had several confrontations with Silva. But the man remained a mystery. Holmberg had made no reference to a Juanito or Juan in his book and I could remember no specific mention of that name in his journal.

By now it was dark and the Indians politely said, "Buenas noches" and returned to their houses about a kilometer upriver. One of the men asked if I would like to visit their settlement in the morning before I left. I told I would try but had no idea how early we would be leaving.

The dinner bell rang and we went to a large table on a screened porch at the side of the main building. The table was filled with men, most of them ranch hands. The two men who had accompanied me in the canoe were there but neither the woman who had brought us nor the boatman. I sat down next to the only other woman in the room, the administrator's wife, Dora. When the meal had been served, I asked her about the woman we came with.

Dora casually said they had decided to go on upriver. "What?" I almost choked. "They left us?" Antonio put down his fork and scrutinized me carefully for a moment. Then he shrugged his shoulders and said we would find something in the morning.

After dinner we talked for a while and then everyone went off to bed. I picked up my sleeping bag, mosquito net, and knapsack and asked Dora where I would sleep. She motioned me to follow and I was led into a large room full of men sleeping on beds or mats on the floor.

"Here?" I have always prided myself on being able to adjust to almost any situation, but spending the night in the men's bunkhouse was out of the question. Dora must have seen the stricken look on my face.

"Aren't you the woman of one of the two men you came with? I thought you would want to be with them."

"No. I don't know who they are. They just happened to be in the same canoe. I don't even know where they're going."

Dora scrutinized me just as her husband had done at the table. She apologized for the misunderstanding and took me to her thatched house where I was given a spare bed.

I was up early in the morning, concerned about continuing upriver. The administrator told me he would take us to another settlement where we could probably hire a boat. First, however, he had to make a quick trip to El Carmen for some supplies. He had a fast aluminum jon boat and said he would be back by 10 or so.

With several hours to fill, I decided to visit the Indians. Dora said she would like to come so we started down the trail. The two men caught up with us and told us they would also like to see the Sirionó camp. I wasn't enthusiastic but said nothing.

The Sirionó settlement consisted of four thatched houses in a small clearing. Six families lived there. The houses were mostly open with a few woven palm branches offering protection from wind and rain. I saw my first Sirionó string hammock slung under one of the palm shelters. An old man with short, cropped hair came forward to greet me. He was dressed in ragged pants and a shirt with no buttons. In spite of his tattered appearance he carried himself erect and held out his hand in welcome.

"I am Jêjê, the cacique"

"I am pleased to meet you Jêjê. I am pleased to meet a Sirionó ererecua." His eyes sparkled when I used his Sirionó title. He took me to each house and introduced the people there. All six families were related by blood or marriage. By now the two men had become bored and decided to walk back to the ranch house. Dora was also eager to return, finding nothing interesting in what she later described as "a few dirty Indians living in hovels." But I wanted to spend some time with Jêjê, knowing this would probably be my only opportunity to meet and talk with the old man. Dora didn't want to go back alone, so she found a log in the shade and sat there brushing away mosquitoes with a branch while I continued to visit with Jêjê. The old ererecua told me that at one time there were quite a few Sirionó living on the Richards ranch. For a number of years, the missionary I had met briefly in Gainesville, Perry Priest, and his wife, Anne, had lived there periodically with the Indians. Jêjê told me that many of those left at San Pedro were considering leaving for Ibiato where they had relatives. The major impediment to moving was indebtedness to the ranch owners. Unless the debt was paid, the Indians would be fugitives if they left. Jêjê tole me that Perry had been able to help some of the Sirionó by paying off their debts. These had gone to Ibiato. Jêjê himself had thought of leaving, but said that he liked living on the Río Blanco and was too old to start a new life someplace else. Jêjê also told me he had been with a Sirionó band contacted by Silva and Holmberg north of Yaguarú. Like the old Austrian nun, the episode was just a fleeting moment in the old man's life and he could give me few details.

I went back to the house with Dora, gathered my belongings and was ready to leave when her husband pulled up in the jon boat. As soon as the ranch supplies were unloaded, the two men and I climbed aboard and were whisked upriver to another settlement. I marveled at the speed of the aluminum boat pushed along by the large outboard motor, covering in just a few minutes the same distance it would take hours to travel by canoe. At the settlement, Antonio took us to talk to a man with a boat and motor. Again, I noted a real reluctance to help us. I found this uncooperative attitude contrary to anything I had experienced in the lowlands and began to wonder what was going on. The boatman complained that gasoline was scarce and that he wasn't certain he could find any. At this point the two men began to discuss their reasons for going upriver—to buy macaws to resell in Trinidad. This was the first time I heard either of them discuss the nature of their journey. The boatman just grunted and then looked at me.

"I'm trying to reach a man named Luís Silva Sánchez. I want to write about his experiences with the Chori." I hated using "Chori" but knew that very likely he would be unfamiliar with the term Sirionó. I also realized that if I didn't manage to convince this man of the importance of my trip, I would never get to Las Piedras. "I have come all the way from the United States just to find Luís Silva Sánchez." A gross exaggeration, but I was getting desperate. A small smile crossed the boatman's face.

"Everyone along the river knows Lucho," he said, using the nickname for Luís; "his stories of the Chori are famous."

Then the boatman turned to the two men and told them he would take them upriver for U.S. $30, an exorbitant price. I sat still, not saying a word. The two men tried to get the price down, but the boatman stood fast on his first offer. Finally, the two men got up, told Antonio they would be going back to El Carmen and walked back to the jon boat. Antonio asked me if I was coming too. I said, "No." No matter what the price, I would get to Las Piedras. He shrugged his shoulders and left.

I turned to the boatman who was now grinning from ear to ear. I looked at him in surprise. "Those men are not parrot buyers," he said. "They're *forestales*, forestry agents. Word about them has spread all along the river. They come here to confiscate our birds and then they sell them for their own profit. They are nothing but thieves working for the government which is the biggest thief of all! Now, let me get the boat and we will hurry. The canoe that left you last night is upstream but I think we can catch up with them."

In less than an hour we stopped at another *barraca*, or homestead, on the high bank of the river. The canoe I left El Carmen in was tied to a post by the steep, muddy incline. We climbed to the top where we saw several people, including the occupants of the canoe, sitting in the shade drinking coffee. They stared at us in silence as we crossed the small, swept courtyard. I said, "Buenas tardes," and received an unenthusiastic reply from the coffee drinkers. I stood back and let the boatman approach them. He shook hands all around and began talking. I strained to overhear what he was telling them but could only catch snatches of the conversation. Every few seconds eyes would dart my way and then back to the boatman. Finally, the boatman beckoned me over. I was given a chair and brought a cup of thick, black, very sweet coffee. I took a sip, said the proper things, and everyone seemed to relax. Again, I repeated my story of looking for Silva to write about his experiences. The lowland hospitality I had mysteriously been denied was once again in evidence. A hammock was brought for me to rest in. A meal was prepared which I ate greedily in front of my pleased hosts. Gringos had been that way before, I was told, and had scorned offers of food and drink, preferring to prepare their own. When we were ready to leave, I was presented with six fresh eggs and two large cakes of hard brown sugar called *empanizado*. I was embraced by each member of the family and escorted to the canoe amid pleas to return again soon.

The afternoon was beautiful. The blue, cloudless sky set off the greenness of the foliage around us and gave the river a smooth, almost oily look. The little two-horsepower engine barely pushed us upstream, making no wake. I sat in the bow atop bags of supplies and wedged up against my knapsack. Hour after hour, the motor droned on. It began to get dark, and I found myself asking, "Is it much farther?"

We lost the last bit of light but still continued upstream. The boatman got out an old, weak flashlight to navigate by. Taking his cue, I reached into my knapsack and pulled out my light with its fresh batteries and strong, steady beam.

CHAPTER THREE

"Good," he said, "just sweep the river slowly, back and forth, so I can see where the banks are and if there are any snags." The sky was clear but there was no moon. I tried to brace myself in case we hit something. I also had one hand through my knapsack strap in the event the canoe overturned. The backpack probably would float for awhile and I didn't want to end up washed ashore with no knife, mosquito net, or worst of all, my butane lighter.

Finally, my flashlight beam caught the shape of some large, round rocks sticking out of the water. This was the only outcropping of stone I had seen along the river and at first I wasn't certain what it was.

"That's it," the boatman said, "Las Piedras. We're here." As we tied up the canoe I looked around for some sign of habitation, a house or a light. But there was nothing. Sensing my uneasiness the boatman explained that we would have to walk inland about half a kilometer. Silva had not built his house right on the river.

I followed him along a narrow trail to a clearing. I could make out the shape of several houses and what seemed like a bamboo fence. We followed the fence to a gate and walked into the inner courtyard. There was a kerosene wick lamp burning in one of the houses.

The boatman called out, "Hay gente? Is anyone there?" A stout figure approached us, carrying the lamp. I could see it was an older woman. She told me she was Silva's wife. I said I had come to interview her husband about his life. At this, the boatman took his leave, would accept no payment, and went on his way another kilometer or so upstream. Silva's wife, Clemencia, took me into the palm-thatched house. It consisted of an open-porch with a sleeping room behind. When Clemencia went into the back room, I could see two hammocks hanging, one empty, one occupied. She spoke gently to the person in the hammock and then came out to ask me if I were hungry or would I just like some coffee? I said coffee would be fine. Clemencia went off to another building across the courtyard and I could hear her fanning the embers of the cooking fire. At that moment a large, robust man with gray-streaked hair stepped into the lamplight from the room beyond. In the low light I couldn't see his face well except to note he wore glasses and didn't seem as old as he was reported to be.

"I am Luís Silva. How may I be of service?" The casualness of his greeting caught me unprepared. I was tired, sunburned, and emotionally drained from the efforts of reaching this place. Now that I was finally face to face with Holmberg's guide, I wasn't certain where to begin. At that moment, Doña Clemencia brought me a cup of hot coffee which quickly began to revive me.

Silva was visibly impressed that I had come all that way just to talk to him. My very first reaction to the man was probably relief. I knew he must be in his seventies, and I was worried that, like the priest Hildebert, he would no longer remember much of his past. To my delight Silva was

34

not only lucid but had a phenomenal memory. He began a steady stream of talk about himself, Holmberg, and the Sirionó, stopping only momentarily to produce a signed copy of Holmberg's dissertation. My fatigue began to get the best of me; Silva's words were floating around me like a fog. I interrupted to tell him that I was very tired and that I didn't want to miss any of what he was relating. Could we tape it all in the morning? He smiled apologetically and said, yes, we could start first thing. Doña Clemencia brought me a big, wide Brazilian hammock to sleep in. It took only a few moments to rig my mosquito net, unroll my sleeping bag, and crawl in.

Long before dawn I was awakened by the pounding of a *tacú* (mortar) somewhere behind my head. I listened for a moment and could tell by the rhythm and the raspy sound that rice was being hulled. But why so early? I hit the button on my watch that lighted the face: 4:15 a.m. The pounding continued. I pulled my sleeping bag over my head and dozed off. Then the chickens began to move around and a dog barked. I uncovered my head and discovered that the pitch blackness of the night had given way to gray dawn. People were up and about and I could smell food cooking. Silva was standing in the middle of the courtyard holding an old tin cup and brushing his teeth. I walked across the patio to greet him and was immediately struck by the youthful appearance of the man. He was quite tall, had a full head of hair cut quite long so that it fell over his ears, and his face had a tanned, healthy look. He smiled and apologized for the noise earlier.

"One of my sons just left on a hunting trip and food had to be made ready," he explained. I smiled and nodded. Doña Clemencia motioned us over to a table which had been set up in the same area where I had slept. After an ample breakfast, the table was cleared and Don Luís and I sat down to begin his story. I turned on my tape recorder.

"Luís Silva Sánchez"

"Jêjê"

FOUR
Chapter 4

"Doctora, my life reads like a novel. I was born in Santa Cruz in 1906. I didn't know a father. At the age of five my mother brought me to the Beni, to the capital, Trinidad, where I was brought up. Unfortunately, I didn't have a father but I had a stepfather who treated me very badly. I was never allowed to go to school. I was born only to work. For that reason I have little formal education. I was a peon in my own house, that's all.

"An uncle of mine came by one day, my mother's brother, and I begged him to take me away from that place. He more or less understood my situation. So, this uncle took me to an *estancia* called 'Cocharca,' where we worked a couple of years and then we went to a place near San Ramón del Iténez, called the Iturupuru River, and the settlement is called 'Esperanza.' At that time there was an old man there, Don Manan Aguilera, who said to me, 'Son, you haven't learned anything, they haven't taught you anything in Trinidad except the whip. Good, well now we are going to find a way, a night school.' So, three of us entered the school, with the help of the owner of the ranch, an Argentine named Don Agustín Moreno. My uncle was his administrator. This man had his son, Aureliano, who was very spoiled because he was an only child. He couldn't send him to the capital [Trinidad] to study because he would be all alone there with no one to care for him... and he had a boy he raised who was from the region of Chiquitos who was called Leónida Atipobo and he was the companion of Don Agustin's son, Aureliano, who was my friend too. So, they talked to this old man Aguilera who agreed to teach us at night. Then a victrola arrived and we would take it out behind the house to listen to it instead of going to school. We were finally discovered and punished. We went back to school but it was very poor schooling. All we had for light was an old clay pot which burned alligator fat, and an old ruin of a house. But we did our best. Since his father was rich, Aureliano went on to study and eventually became a veterinarian. Leónida and I went our own ways. So unfortunately all the education I have was that small night school.

"Then I went to live with my mother again. By now I was a young man and my mother had cattle so we moved to Trinidad. My stepfather, Ezequial Susano, had been killed by his own nephew. This is public knowledge, everyone in Trinidad knows about it. He left my mother earlier for a younger woman. So my mother gathered up her cattle and with my uncle they bought a small ranch near Trinidad. Then we bought a house in the city and I moved there with my mother. At that time the war [Chaco War] had started and I was drafted by General Federico Román. My mother fought very hard to get me out of the army because she was poor, a widow, and I was her only son. But General Román himself told her I was needed at the front to defend the homeland. So, my mother, crying, gave me her blessing and told me, 'What else can we do, son? You will go, but don't desert. God is great.' I went to the war and thank God, I returned, but with a broken arm...not from a bullet but when a truck went over a cliff between Villa Montes and Tarija. There were twenty-some of us on the truck and only six of us survived. When the hostilities ceased, twenty-one of us were brought by truck to Santa Cruz. From there I had no way back to the Beni. But I ran into an old neighbor of mine who also had been mobilized, a one-eyed man named Pacífico Lijerón. So I said, 'OK, brother, we'll go together.' 'But man,' he says, 'what about the savages in the forest at Quebrada Blanca? They'll attack us.' 'No, *hombre*, we are the savages! I know the trail well and have traveled it many times and they've never attacked. Let's go!' Our only weapon was a penknife I had. We came all the way on foot until we were eight leagues [40 kilometers] from Trinidad at a place called San Andrés where I knew I could find my mother. But my mother wasn't there. She had gone to Trinidad thinking I would be returning with the troops coming by way of the Ichilo River by raft. When she couldn't find me she began to ask around. One of the men she spoke to was Francisco Asogue, who as a matter of fact was the man who pulled me out of the ravine after the truck accident and knew I was alive. Thinking to play a joke on me, he told my mother I had died in the accident. In the meantime, I started out to find my mother in Trinidad. Along the trail, a man told me she was only about two kilometers away, coming on an ox cart. I decided to hide in the trees and surprise her as she passed by. When I came out of the woods she fell off the ox cart in a dead faint. I picked her up and spoke to her. She threw her arms around me and cried for a long time.

"That night the village of San Andrés gave me a big welcoming fiesta and we all got very drunk. Well, when I went off to war, I didn't think I would ever be back so I sold my few head of cattle and everything else. I didn't have anything, no money, nothing. I began to take my mother's cattle, one at a time, and slaughter them to get money...mostly to gamble and drink with my friends. During this time there was a very fat, tame cow that everyone wanted to buy off my mother, offering her two cows in exchange. But she wouldn't sell. I took the cow and sold it without her knowledge...and that same day the butcher slaughtered it. Then they told my mother that her cow had been slaughtered. The cow even had a name, 'La Niña' [little girl]. My mother found me and asked, 'Why did you sell La Niña?' I couldn't find any words and put my head down. Then my mother grabbed a stick and beat me. I was mad and went off to drink with my friends. My cousin's husband was there, Adolfo Vaca, and he told me that he was employed at a new settlement called Casarabe and the director was Don Carlos Loayza Beltrán, married to Cilia Soruco of San Carlos. [I interrupted here to tell him that I had worked in the village of San Carlos as a Peace Corps volunteer and knew Cilia's family there.]

"At that time, this Loayza Beltrán had a brother who was a government minister. Don Carlos knew that some Indians [Sirionó] had come out at a place near Casarabe that is called Buen Jesús. So, Don Carlos and his wife decided to form a nucleo for these Indians [I suspect that Carlos Loayza, who had worked as a newspaperman, was aware of Cándido Mariano de Silva Rondón's well-publicized successes in Brazil using nonviolent methods to contact the Nambiquara Indians and decided to attempt the same in Bolivia.] He founded this nucleo, bringing the Sirionó from Buen Jesús to Casarabe. They were tame, however, not wild. He received help from the government through his brother who was a minister in the government. I don't remember exactly what year this was, but right after the war, about 1937–38.

"Well, my cousin's husband told me he was working for Loayza Beltrán earning 2,000 bolivianos a month and why didn't I come along with him? Then my mother found out I was going to Casarabe and began to cry, 'Son, why are you leaving me? You are my only son. Who will take care of the cattle?' I told my mother that if I stayed I would probably finish off all her cattle one by one. My mother threw up her hands and said, 'Even the war hasn't straightened you out!' Frankly I was pretty wild in those days, drinking and carousing. I sang, played the guitar, flute, and drum, and everyone wanted me at their parties. So I left.

"When I got there, Director Loayza told me there weren't any openings. I told him I would do any type of work and I didn't have to be on the official payroll. The director again said, 'There is no vacancy; all I could pay you is 150 bolivianos a month.' 'Whatever, it doesn't matter. I just want to work,' I responded. Then Director Loayza handed me over to the head of the carpentry shop. Well, I worked there for about a month as a sawyer. Then some of the Indians ran away. It was April, and they would always run away in April or May. No one could figure out why. But then, they made them work too hard, really too hard, and they weren't accustomed to it. Anyway, there was a Peruvian there. He left Peru because of some political problems and ended up in Casarabe working for Loayza. So, he was told to go out and look for the Indians who had fled to the forest. In the carpentry I told this man, Balcázar, 'If you want to catch up with those Indians you had better take me along because you don't know anything about the wilderness.' He laughed and went and told the director. Loayza called me to his office and asked me if I wanted to go along to help. I told him that I did, that I wanted to accompany the 'comisión', that I wanted to do something that mattered.

"We started out, but the Peruvian got sick on me after three days. He wasn't used to all the thorns and high grass and all the discomforts we suffered. We had taken along three Indians as our guides. Then I told Balcázar I would take two of the Indians with me and the third could take him to a nearby ranch belonging to a Sr. Añez. So that's what we did. I left him there with one of the Indians while the other two and I continued on. We came to a cutover area that belonged to the Indians we were following.

"It turns out that the reason these Indians fled each year during the months of April and May is that the animals they hunt are extremely fat then, and the honey is plentiful. Since they couldn't go out to hunt and gather honey in Carsarabe, they had to run away. Very well, we found them gathering *chuchillo* [reed] flowers from which they take the stalk to make arrows, or *uba*. Another 'comisión' was out looking for Indians, led by Alberto Díaz and he came upon the group we found almost at the same time. Alberto then says to me, 'Good, let's tie these Indians by the hands and march them back.' 'No, hombre,' I said to him, 'How can we do that to these people? How will they be able to keep all the mosquitoes off themselves?' But he tied them up and we started back. It was pitch dark and we didn't have any light except for a few burning branches. We hardly walked a kilometer all night long. Anyone knows you can't go through the forest at night but because the bugs wouldn't let us alone, we kept walking. We got to Casarabe with these Indians, and Director Loayza called me to his office. 'Listen, Silva,' he said, 'my congratulations, I didn't think you would do it, you are quite a man.' We had arrived in camp without pants even, since I had taken along only two pairs and the forest finished them off. Then, he told me that I would now earn 200 bolivianos. I thanked him and then we sat down and drank together.

He liked to drink. From then on I was in charge of a group of Indians who would go into the forest to cut wood and palm leaves to build houses.

"Time passed, and I went to work in San Nicolás, a ranch where we had a kind of branch station. A group of Indians had come there and from time to time would hire out to the owner. Loayza wanted to bring them to Casarabe, but the owner, Don Nicolás Mercado wouldn't give up his workers. It turns out that the three administrators sent by Loayza to work with the Indians were all thrown off the place because they would get drunk with them and take advantage of the women. So the director told me, 'Go to San Nicolás, Silva, and see what the problem is.' That same Peruvian, Balcázar, who had gone into the forest with me was at San Nicolás and had tried to abuse the daughter of the *paba* [father, elder], and they had shot him. They had him tied up at San Nicolás. They gave him to me and I brought him to Casarabe. The next day Loayza had me take him to Trinidad where I handed him over to the police. I have never learned what happened to him.

"Then Loayza sent me back to San Nicolás with five Indians. Very well, I was mounted on a riding ox and the Indians were on foot with their bows and arrows. The director was to come along after us in a day or two, to talk to Don Nicolás, the owner of the ranch. I knew the old man was difficult so instead of going to the hacienda, we stopped at a renter's farm about a kilometer away to wait for Loayza. The renter was harvesting rice and since the Indians and I had very little food with us, we helped the man harvest his rice so he would feed us. We were there a month. Finally, one day I went up to see Don Nicolás. We struck it off well, but he didn't like Loayza and called him a *Kolla pícaro* [shifty highlander] and other such names. After I had lunch, I told him I was going back to Casarabe, since Loayza hadn't shown up. As we were crossing a pampa on our way back to the nucleo, low and behold, here comes Loayza with eight of his men, all mounted on horses and oxen.

" 'Why are you returning?' he said to me, angry.

" 'Well, director, you said you would meet me here and you never showed up.'

" 'I'm sorry, but things came up. What is this Mercado like? Is he intelligent?'

" 'Yes, he is very intelligent. But he says if you come to his house he will chase you out with a broom.'

" 'Is that so. We'll see.'

"As we rode toward San Nicolás, a terrible surazo hit. We were cold and miserable when we got to Mercado's door. Loayza sent me first since I knew the man. He invited us right in and we all sat down and began to drink and chat. Loayza and Mercado talked on and on, covering every topic imaginable, but never even mentioning Indians. Since it was so cold, Sr.

Mercado had more drinks made, this time hot tea with alcohol. When everyone was well 'warmed up,' only then did Loayza bring up the subject of Indians. But Mercado related the stories of Balcázar and the others and how they had treated the Indians very badly. 'If this is the type of employee you have, what am I to expect of anyone else you send here?' he said. 'No,' assured Loayza, 'I am going to leave you one who is responsible, one who will be under your vigilance. You will be the second director here.' Everything was settled finally, so we continued drinking until about 2 a.m. when we went to bed. No one could sleep very well because of the incredible cold.

"In the morning, Sr. Mercado invited us all to breakfast. After we ate, Mercado got a pencil and notebook and said to Loayza, 'All right, I want to know who will be the man you are going to leave here.' Loayza looked at me and said, 'Silva here.' I stood up and asked Loayza for permission to speak.

" 'I would like to resign.' I said. 'If you had asked me to come here before all this had happened, I would have done so gladly. But now, I would rather just resign from my post.' Then Sr. Mercado looked at me and winked, indicating that I should stay. All of his workers agreed that I should be the one to do the job. So, I gave in, sat down, and decided to stay.

"Well, Mercado gave me a pair of cows each month for the Indians, but they didn't need them really since they hunted all the time. I asked Mercado if I could pay for my pension at his house since I had nowhere to eat and sleeping was impossible in the houses of the Indians, they were like pigsties. 'Fine,' he said. 'But you aren't going to pay me anything. Another plate of food is nothing. When you hear the drumbeat calling the ranch hands, just come and eat.'

"But on the first day, since the Indians lived a kilometer away and I was busy working, I couldn't come to breakfast or lunch. I remained there working, tearing down the old shelter, cutting wood and palm thatch to make a new one, cleaning up. There were thirty families of Indians and they knew how to work well by now. So we thatched, cleaned up, and even began a little house for me to live in. When night came, I went up to the ranch. My breakfast, lunch, and supper plates were all covered and waiting. 'Silva,' said Mercado, 'You have no one here waiting on you!' 'No,' said Doña Aida, his wife, 'Don't be angry at him, he has been working hard.' After dinner Mercado and I talked. He told me he was pleased with my work and since I had told him to keep the two cows because the Indians had plenty of meat he told me he would give them to me. 'You deserve them,' he said. Then he told me that they slaughtered beef every three days and if we ever needed meat, just ask.

"So, I continued working. We put everything in order. We even opened up a road to the ranch that was so clean you could have seen a rabbit on it from a kilometer away. After a few days when my house was finished I told Mercado and his wife that I would no longer be staying with them. 'Is that possible,' he said, 'that you have done all this so quickly? Tomorrow my wife and I will ride over to have a look.' 'Fine,' I said, 'we'll be waiting.'

"At nine the next morning he was there with his wife and little boy. He looked around, tried out some benches I had made and walked around the Indians' large shelter, everything in order. He walked over to me, embraced me and told me that I truly cared about the Indians. 'This is beautiful,' remarked Sra. Aida, 'because before it was a pigsty! Why don't we go up to the house?' That night all of the ranchers came and with the workers we had a big party to celebrate.

"I was there three months. Then a woman I had left in Casarabe came looking for me and began to make trouble. I went to Casarabe to tell Loayza I was leaving the project because this woman was constantly chasing after me. 'No,' he told me. 'We need you.' We sat down to drink. 'I have something else in mind. There are still a great many Indians over by the Río Blanco. I want you to head up a commission and go over there and set up another station, near El Carmen.' [At this point in Silva's story I interrupted to ask him if he had learned to speak Sirionó.] By now I understood quite a bit, I could carry on a conversation. There was an old man named Embuta, or Embutami, which means he only had one hair on his chin. He was an old man who always went around naked. I had met him on the commission to San Pablo. When I returned to Casarabe, he came looking for me. We sat down on the ground and began to talk. Then I saw him look over my shoulder. When I turned around, Loayza was standing there, listening.

" 'Oh, Silva,' he said, 'I, the director, don't even know what you do. I congratulate you for having taken an interest in the language.'

" 'Well, director, since I am alone with them a great deal, I have had to learn because many times I am working with Indians who don't know Spanish.'

"And how did I learn? When they sent me out the first time to cut thatch here I didn't know anything; I was afraid of the Indians who all had axes and machetes. I ran, and they ran after me, no? I was afraid they'd cut me up. I was new there and didn't know anything. So we got to the place where we would cut *motacú* palm. One of the men was called Catana, he seemed 'nobler' than the rest. So I sat down on a log telling myself that today I would learn all the names for motacú. I took a motacú fruit and pointed at it. 'What is this,' I said, and pointed at Catana. 'Yucuri,' he answered. I peeled off the skin and pointed to the fruit inside. 'Eke, yucuri eke.' They speak like in English, backward, no? Yucuri eke. I studied the motacú that day, the whole thing. That's how I began. One by one, I learned the names of things, even the most insignificant. I studied Sirionó and I learned it. So, he says to me, 'Not even I, the director, know what you know.' That night when all the Indians were gathered for class, Loayza told me I would get up and speak to them in Sirionó. The applause of Sirionó turned out to be a whistle, like we do to make fun of someone. So, I stood up in the circle of Indians and began to speak what I knew of their language. They all started whistling. [Silva imitated the Sirionó by emitting a shrill, high-pitched whistle, and then laughed at himself.]

"So it was. When I got ready to go to the Río Blanco I traveled with two companions: Adolfo Gutiérrez, the one who committed suicide, and a Molina; and with several Indians we went to the canton of El Carmen. Many tribes had been brought from this zone to Casarabe but they would run away and go back to the Río Blanco. We set up our station on a ranch, but the owner made the Indians run away and I would have to go after them. By now I was alone, so I founded Tibaera which means *asahi* palm in Sirionó. Once I had the Indians established at Tibaera, I would take them to Casarabe since Tibaera was just a branch station, right?

"When there was only one tribe left in the forest, word was sent to me that I had been fired. The director was really nothing but a thief. For some time now I had been earning 2,000 bolivianos a month. After I was let go and went over to collect my six months in back salary, the director told me I wasn't an 'official' employee, so he couldn't pay me.

"So I stayed over here with four Sirionó men. I knew where the last tribe was, so I decided to go after them and civilize them so they could help me work my own place. We founded Chapacura, farther upstream from Tibaera on the boundary between the Beni and Santa Cruz. In Chapacura the army ants ran me out so I moved here with my people to Las Piedras. I founded a school, went to Santa Cruz and brought out a teacher, Doña Pastora Julio. I put my children and the Indians' in school. She got very ill and died here, so I brought another, Don Ignacio, Ignacio...I don't remember his last name but he was from Magdalena...a good teacher, paid from my own pocket. I ended up having to throw him out, however, because he was after all the girls in his class. By now the Ministry of Education had decided to give us a line item so we were sent a teacher and the Escuela Las Piedras was founded. The school went on for several years; the Indian children were educated, but as soon as they learned to read and write, they left me. They went to Santa Cruz, everywhere, even Argentina. All I have left is Eaboco, an old woman, and her daughter, this woman here. That is the payment these Indians have given me. Once I civilized and educated them, they left me all alone. I have become old struggling with these Indians. Truly, I tell you they were a filthy race in their primitive times. All they had was a string hammock with a fire underneath and filth all around. And they got sick, a lot of tuberculosis, because they had no clothes. I brought a doctor here and medicines were sent from Santa Cruz for the Indians. But they all left me. So here we are, my wife and I, living in this rustic little hut. But since I am in my last days I believe very little time remains until my "Manacos" [a Bolivian brand of shoes] are tied together, as they say. I am just fine. My children are grown and educated the best I knew how. They have done well. I have done my job with them. I have also done well by my country, taking these people out of the wilderness and civilizing them. I have worked with many tribes and it has been written down in books like the one by Dr. Holmberg.

"Now, let me tell you about Holmberg. I had traveled from here, from Tibaera, to Casarabe. I arrived in Casarabe and the director, Loayza, tells me, 'A gringo has come here, from the United States. This gringo is a real ox, he doesn't even speak Spanish; but according to his papers, he is someone important, a writer or something. But he doesn't speak a word and he smells like a *cepe* [leaf-cutter ant].' At that time, you know, we had no experience with mosquito repellant which Holmberg had brought along. 'I'll take you over there so you can meet him.'

"We left the office and walked over to Holmberg's house. The gringo was sitting on a chair in the house he had had made there in Casarabe. He was very young, handsome, and fair; but we went in and he didn't even say 'good day' to the director nor did the director greet him. I did the same since they told me he couldn't understand Spanish. 'Well, do your best with him, even if it's with sign language,' the director told me, 'I'm leaving you here.' And he went back to his office. Holmberg's gaze followed the director. Holmberg had a lot of equipment in his room, good equipment. I said to myself, 'This is a man of wealth.' Then he began to open some bags and took out a flashlight, a pocket knife, a belt, and some pearl necklaces and put them in my hands. When I started to give these things back, he stopped me and made a sign that they were for me to keep. I thanked him. 'But what a shame,' I thought, 'that this man can't understand me, nor I him.' Under a table there was a can of local alcohol and he made a sign to ask if I wanted a drink. So, Dr. Holmberg got out two tin cups and filled them with alcohol and water. It was about 3 or 4 in the afternoon. We sat there and drank in silence. At about 5, one of the Sirionó children came to tell me that the director wanted me at the office. 'All right, I'll be right there,' I told him.

"I sat down my cup and signaled to Holmberg that I would be right back. He grabbed my hand and motioned for the child to leave. Then he shut the door. We had already had a cup or two so we were pretty 'warmed up.' He says to me, 'Don't go.' Just as I had thought! How could this man have come all the way to Bolivia without knowing any Spanish? 'Don't go, he's the ox, not me,' he said, grabbing my nose and shaking it [a riding ox is guided by a nose ring]. 'Look, Silva, I have come here and I now know everyone. All of them, including the director, are nothing but a bunch of *pícaros*, thieves and rogues who cheat the Indians. I gave them gifts and the mestizos took them away from them. I want to go to the Río Blanco, to El Carmen with you. You can't say a word to anyone that I can speak Spanish or that I'm leaving.' We continued drinking. I told him that I lived in a rude hut in the woods and could offer him few amenities. 'No,' he said, 'That's exactly why I came here; I haven't come to be in cities but to be with the Indians like you.' We got very drunk together that night.

"The next morning, I went to the office to see Loayza. 'How'd it go with the gringo?'

" 'We got drunk but you're right, he can't speak a word of Spanish.'

"I spent three days in Casarabe and then Holmberg and I went to Trinidad and we stayed in the best hotel there, the América, which belonged to a Chilean, Don Aguinaldo Zambrana. Holmberg had me a virtual prisoner in that hotel for three days, paying all the bills while I taught him some Sirionó. Then he told me he would meet me in Tibaera in about a month. 'Good,' I said. 'Over there you have a countryman, Don Federico Richards.' So, we said goodbye and I went back to El Carmen and on up to my post at Tibaera. One day I was on my way down from Tibaera and I came to some houses near the Richards' place. Some Guarayos there told me that a gringo had arrived at the Richards' ranch, another American. When I got there, it was Holmberg. He had flown to Magdalena and then came upriver to San Pedro.

"Richards then sent him with a boat and several Sirionó men to Tibaera where he was with me some eight months. During that time we made the trip into the Guarayos missions where he got sick. On that trip, we were looking for the tribe of Ečiba-eoko, long arm.

"I had a companion, whose name is immortalized in a lake nearby, Eresaeanta, hard eye. This was a man who really knew the wilderness, the 'king of the forest.' He lived on the shore of the lake where I found him and I named the lake after him, Eresa-eanta. He had his friend Choño-eke with him because he was an old man and Eresa-eanta couldn't stay long with the big tribe. He had seven wives and the young men were always trying to take them away from him, so he stayed away. I found both of them and the women in the forest and took them to Chiquiguani where I was first before I founded Tibaera. It was a continual battle there over the women. Eresa-eanta told me he was taking his women back into the forest where he had some *yuca* [manioc] planted and they left. When Holmberg and I got ready to go to the Guarayos region, I found Eresa-eanta and got him to come with us because he was the best man around. We went into the virgin forest of the Río Blanco. It was difficult work. They [the Sirionó] don't stay put. They build a hut called a *tuyua*, of piled-up motacú fronds. When the hunting got bad, they would move on to another place. They were nomads. So, one would come to an abandoned tuyua and from there try to find their trail. Eresa-eanta knew that when they went out hunting early in the morning, they would light dry motacú fronds to see by. When it got light, these would be thrown off to the side of the trail. We would come across these and know we were not far from the camp. Right there we left our packs, everything, and we took off our clothes because Eresa-eanta told us that just as we were upset by seeing people naked, the Sirionó were upset by seeing people with clothes on. We got to Ečiba-eoko's tribe. I don't remember exactly... but the tribe consisted of about forty or fifty families. And there was a little girl, I remember, that Holmberg said couldn't have been more than thirteen and who had just given birth to a little boy. They were both burning up with high fevers. She had hardly any breasts yet, and had to pull on her skin to let the baby suck. So we left three of our Sirionó companions to lead the group back to Tibaera while we went ahead to look for the tribe of two old deaf brothers... Iza and Yocoi. Iza means deaf and Yocoi means termite. So we continued. We caught up with the tribe, but many of them were old or had clubfeet, so we did not try to send them to Tibaera. Yocoi said they were too old to travel that far. While we were in this camp, Holmberg came down with a bad infection in both eyes. He was gravely ill, and I worried about him because he carried a shotgun. One day we came to an abandoned house and when I let go of his arm he ran into a post which hit him in the face. He grabbed his machete, and blind, began swinging at the post which he missed because he couldn't see it. Then he shouted this word which sounds something like 'Shet!' I was afraid, and said to myself, 'This gringo could kill himself and people will think I did it,' because he carried around a large package of money, some dollars, some bolivianos.

"So, I told Holmberg we would try to get to Yaguarú, the Guarayo mission, to find him some medical assistance. We didn't have anything at all with us to treat him... absolutely nothing... so I led him by the hand with my friend, Eresa-eanta, breaking trail ahead for us.

"One day we came out on a large burned-over field belonging to the Guarayos that the Sirionó call turuquia, or bare pampa. I tell you, every time we passed a sunny spot in the forest, Holmberg would cry out in pain because the light made his eyes hurt terribly. 'Listen,' I told him, 'we have to cross a field here, a pampa.' 'Just a minute,' he said. He sat down, bent over and closed his eyes. 'How far do we have to go to cross the pampa?'

"I calculated about two kilometers, but I told him about one kilometer... in the sun. It was about 10 or 11 in the morning. 'OK,' he said, 'let me rest just a minute.' When he was ready, I took him by the hand and we started out. Just at about the place where we had come a kilometer, he asked me if we were almost at the edge of the forest so he could rest his eyes.

I told him just a little bit farther. Finally, we came to the forest and he sat down, pushing away my hand with anger and not speaking to me. Then he said that word again, 'shet.' After a few minutes he spoke to me and said, 'You lied to me, we've come more than two kilometers.' 'Well,' I told him, 'that may be true. But the truth is I'm no engineer to appreciate distances; I calculated more or less a kilometer.' 'Yes!' he said, 'we've walked more than two kilometers. You lied to me!' He was cleaning the pus from his eyes. I kept silent then.

"After an hour's rest, we started out again, circling a large lake and crossing some more forest. Then I called on Eresa-casi, who belonged to the tribe of Iza and Yocoi, because he knew that area well. He was what they call an *uru ue*. This Indian had raped his mother; and when we got to his tribe, he lived apart in his own shelter, something unknown among the Sirionó who always live in a common dwelling. I asked an old woman there why he lived apart and she said because he was an uru ue, a wooden ear, he doesn't hear or understand. 'He's an uru ue.' 'Why is he an uru ue?' I asked. She told me he was crazy, someone who doesn't understand, and who had raped his mother. 'He's a crazy man, *paripari*,' she said. The man whispered in his mother's ear that he had killed an *anta* [tapir]. He even left his bamboo point arrow in the forest so she would believe him. Then he told her to bring her *panacú* [a woven palm backpack] to bring the meat back. He sent his mother on ahead, she was still a young woman, and then he followed after her and raped her there in the woods. There was no anta. When he got back he was beaten with sticks and made to build his shelter apart, his tuyua.

"Very well, since this man was apart from his tribe I spoke to him about coming with us to the Guarayos and he accepted. Four days out, we got to some Guarayo chacos that he was familiar with. Then we came to some fields of *plátanos* [plantains] and yuca. In one of these fields we came upon an old guarayo couple pulling yuca. This was the last day of Yaguarú's fiesta for its patron saint. Eresa-eanta, who always went ahead, motioned to me, pointing out the two Guarayos. They were drunk from the fiesta and had come out to pull a little yuca to cook and eat. We were about five kilometers from Yaguarú. When the Guarayos saw us, they tried to flee because the Indians with us were naked. Since I speak quite a bit of Guaraní I called to them...'*erio che caray*' I told them, 'come here, I am *carayona*, people [not a "savage"].' Then they came over, shaking, because they were really afraid. They took us to the mission administration.

"Arriving at the mission, now in the last day of its fiesta, the Indians walked along with three armadillos they had killed hung around their necks. The administrator was a Czech I think...his name was Francisco Materna. But when we walked through town there was a virtual riot when the Guarayos saw us and the naked Indians. Drums and flutes played, people yelled, and everyone was drunk. They surrounded us as we walked toward the administration office. When we got there, the meat the Indians had been carrying had been stolen. We were now completely out of food since our supplies had run out several days before and we had lived on meat only. We had no rice, salt, or lard. Everything was used up. So Holmberg told me to ask Materna for some supplies and he would pay for them. Then we were brought a huge plate of *biscochos* [corn biscuits] and coffee. We finished off the first plate and Holmberg had another brought, until we were full. Then the Czech gave Holmberg the top floor of the building, which was usually reserved for visiting dignitaries. We asked about medical help so Materna sent for one of the two nuns there who was a nurse. This nun was German. She came with all her equipment. Then I told Holmberg that he should leave his money with the nun because the Guarayos are thieves. She took the packet of money I handed her and put it in her skirt. Then she sat down and began to treat him, washing his eyes and putting in some sort of medicine.

"We were there fourteen days, staying in the mission administration compound. A Sunday came along...these people have the custom of bringing a band inside the church to play for Mass. There was a big, long window in the church and when the Indians heard the music, which they weren't familiar with, they all ran to the window and stood up on the sill to see what was happening. When the Guarayo women saw all the naked Sirionó standing up in the window, the church erupted with shouts and giggling. After Mass was over, I asked the Indians what they thought of the instruments. They said that those things that made noise were all twisted, like people with clubfeet. Then I asked them if they liked the music and they said, '*Tei!*, No! We didn't like the music!'

"But now it was costing a lot of money to feed everyone and we were using up the administration's supplies, so I told the Indians to go back to the place where we had met the two old Guarayos pulling yuca and to make a camp there. They could eat and hunt. The group left and two stayed, my campanion, Eresa-eanta, and one other.

"After two weeks or so, Holmberg was well and we left Yaguarú and started back to Tibaera. On the way, we caught up with the first tribe we had sent on back to Tibaera. They were slowly moving along, camping and hunting along the way. About 500 meters before we got to one of their old camps, we came across the bodies of that little girl and her baby. The baby looked like a bat, wrinkled with the skin pulled over his bones. Holmberg lifted the girl's head and said, 'What a pity.' The tribe had abandoned them, but she had dragged herself and her baby along after them to that spot where we found them.

"We left the bodies where they were and went on, eventually catching up with the tribe. The old people were slow, and if they came across a bunch of troop pigs [white-lipped peccaries], they would have to stay there until all the meat had been eaten. Sometimes three or sometimes only two kilometers a day. We continued on to Tibaera with this tribe, Ečiba-eoko's. On the way, I remember I killed fourteen pigs and we had to stay four days to finish the meat. I'll tell you, in the forest, they were the bosses. I, who would become their catequist, could do nothing to impose my ideas on them. They were in their place. I had to do what they told me. For example, many people tease me that I had my way with the Sirionó women. But I didn't, I swear by God. Never! In the first place, after Holmberg left I was alone, and these people have the custom that from birth, a girl has a husband, no? For example, you have a daughter and I am her husband. Then you have another daughter, she is also to be my wife. But I have to help raise her, bring in meat, until she is old enough to live with me. So in the first place, there were no single women. In the second place, since I was alone, if I did anything bad they would have killed me instantly, because they are jealous people. Brothers could share wives, but if it were anyone else, there would be a terrible fight. And when a man was very jealous and mad at his wife, he would come over and cut up her hammock, leaving her to sit there and cry all day. Given all this, how was I to have done what they say? Impossible. I respected the Indians. Of all the tribes I have taken out, all the chiefs liked me. They even let me go into the forest with their women so they could bring back the meat I shot. So, see how they trusted me.

"Then Holmberg received a letter telling him to come to La Paz. There, they told him that he would help collect rubber for the war that had started. He was in charge of this zone. During that time I got my letter from Casarabe telling me I was fired. So I took two of the men with me and went over to Lago Huachi where two Cruceños had wanted me to work rubber. They wanted me to bring the whole tribe with me but I said I couldn't, that I had been just an employee at Tibaera. Another man was sent from Casarabe to administer Tibaera, but in a few days the whole tribe left and came over to Huachi where I was. The administrator left and Tibaera was abandoned. So, Colonel Riva, one of the two Cruceños, told me to go to work with my Indians and I would be paid generously. He was a close friend of the president at that time. But I didn't want to. I preferred to work for myself. The Indians stayed with me at Hauchi. We worked collecting rubber; but it went badly. My people died because it is terrible work. . .and the buyers made all the profit. When I left, I didn't even have any sandals. Holmberg came to Huachi then and gave me some clothes and we went to Guayaramerín, where he had to check on some rubber. We were there three months. Then Frederick Richards' son, Abrahán, took over the contract to deliver rubber to Holmberg. Holmberg wanted me to do it, but I was afraid it might turn out badly so I refused. When Abrahán took the contract, Holmberg asked me to work with Richards because he was pretty young and inexperienced. I agreed. I went and worked rubber with Richards and his people. One day Holmberg came by and told me he was going to Peru and then to the United States. He wanted me to come with him. But I told him, 'What would an old *kimbai* [Sirionó word for man] like me do in the United States?' Holmberg's replacement arrived, another American, a Mr. Graft [Kraft?], and Holmberg presented me to him and told the man, 'I owe my life to this man, please look out for him.' The other gringo took my arm and smiled. Holmberg left and I never saw him again. He sent me many letters from Peru and then from the United States, but I never wrote; I don't know why, he was my best friend. That is how I treated his friendship. The post office here, they just take your letters, open them up, and throw them away. Maybe that's why. In your writing, doctora, I would like to request that you give my condolences to all of Holmberg's family. I would like my sentiments toward him to be known. He was like my brother.

"Well, doctora, that is about all. There is so much more I could tell you, but it would take many days. As I told you, my life has been like a novel!"

"Jack Anderson"

FIVE
Chapter 5

When Silva and I finished taping his story, it was almost lunchtime. We got up and went into the patio to stretch a bit while Clemencia prepared the table.

"Don Luís," I asked, "Do you know someone named Juanito? I think he was connected with the mission at Ibiato."

Silva gave me a quizzical look and a small frown crossed his face.

"Juanito? Sí, Juanito Anderson, the missionary. He founded Ibiato."

Anderson? The name sounded familiar. Then I remembered a letter among Holmberg's Sirionó journals and papers written by a man named Jack Anderson. The name had stuck in my memory because of its well-known counterpart, the investigative reporter. I had assumed "Juanito" meant "Johnny." The other nickname for John, "Jack," simply hadn't occurred to me. Holmberg evidently had written to Anderson about some questions concerning kinship. Anderson's response was among Holmberg's field papers; but other than his signature on the letter, there was nothing else to identify him. Although Holmberg made brief mention of Ibiato in his book, Anderson was not included.

"Is Anderson still alive?" I asked. Like Silva, he would be an old man by now. If he were alive, he would probably be in retirement in the United States.

"Oh yes," Silva responded. "You can find him in Trinidad. He has a couple of churches there, still going strong". Anderson was right there in Trinidad? "How do I find him?" "Everyone who has lived in the city for any length of time knows him. Just ask around. His church is right downtown."

I asked Silva to tell me about Anderson. Silva hesitated and then smiled. They went back a long time, he said, and had been enemies for years. Jack had established the mission at Ibiato about the time Casarabe was operating under Loayza. Jack had grown up in Bolivia and was "good" in the woods. Like Silva, he also would go into the wilderness to track the Sirionó and bring them to Ibiato. Jack hated Casarabe, located only five kilometers from Ibiato, and was always trying to get the Casarabe Indians over to his mission. Silva also noted that Anderson considered the camp a den of iniquity because of the drinking that went on. Ibiato was a fundamentalist mission and no alcohol was permitted in the community. Loayza loathed Anderson's meddling in Casarabe's affairs, and according to Silva, told the missionary one day that if Anderson ever set foot in Casarabe again he would shoot him on sight.

The real enmity between Silva and Anderson did not develop until Silva moved to the Río Blanco to set up Tibaera. The few remaining unacculturated Sirionó bands were located in this region, so Anderson, just as Silva, made frequent trips into the area in search of Indians. The two men began competing for Sirionó. On at least two occasions, Anderson found out that Silva had contacted a group and was bringing it out. Anderson went after them with his own Sirionó men and took the Indians away from Silva at gunpoint. This, I thought, was no typical missionary.

Now that I had found Silva and interviewed him, I had to deal with the problem of my return. Until this moment, the challenge of locating Silva and the excitment of meeting and talking with him had pushed that problem to the back of my mind. After lunch, I broached the subject with Don Luís. He thought a moment, then asked if I could help with the cost of gasoline for his son Esteban's 25-horsepower outboard. Esteban had a girlfriend in El Carmen whom he hadn't seen for awhile. Silva called his son to the house and we discussed the plan. I gave Esteban some money so he could go upriver to another settlement where he thought he could buy a few liters of gas.

Within the hour he was back. We loaded the canoe with rice and plantains to be sold in El Carmen. I took leave of Luís Silva and his family, and we headed downstream with a roar. Moving with the current, not against it, and with the big motor, we fairly flew down the river. Esteban told me it would be 9 or 10 that night before we reached El Carmen, but considering how long it had taken me to get to Las Piedras, this trip would be fast.

The river seemed monotonous since I had nothing to look forward to. As I dwelled on the problem of getting back to Trinidad, my anxiety mounted. Traveling on the far side of the river, we passed San Pedro de Richards at dusk. I looked across at the ranch and saw a man sitting on a huge log by the water. He wore no clothes and his wet skin glistened in the fading sunlight. His arms were extended behind him, supporting his weight as he leaned back with his head turned toward the horizon. He reminded me of some great waterbird, wings outspread as it preened in the sun. It was Jêjê. I waved, but he didn't respond. He was lost in his own world. For an instant, I had a glimpse of what once had been.

When it got dark, I repeated sweeping the river with my flashlight as I had done the night before. Since we were moving much faster, I could only hope that Esteban knew the river well. We arrived at El Carmen at 9:45 p.m., as promised and I could see lanterns in the houses as we unloaded the canoe. Esteban walked me to Neyla's house, I thanked him for his help, and he left. Neyla was surprised to see me back so soon. She told me I was lucky to have found someone with a big boat and motor who was willing to make the trip at my convenience. I agreed. She fed me some bread and coffee, and we went to bed.

The next morning I was awakened by the sound of the generator and a shortwave radio. Neyla was talking to someone. At breakfast she told me the town's annual *fiesta patronal* would be starting in a few days and that some people, relatives it seems, had hired a plane to bring them out. The express flight was costing them about U.S. $120. They would arrive around noon and had asked Neyla to see if she could find anyone interested in flying to Trinidad on the pilot's return trip to help defray the cost of the flight. Three people could go for U.S. $20 each.

I leaped at the opportunity. At 11:30 we walked down to the airstrip and waited. A single-engine plane landed a few minutes later. Neyla explained that the flight had already been paid for in Trinidad, so I would give my money to the woman who had hired the plane. I gave her a $20 bill, which delighted her. The rate of inflation was so bad in Bolivia that people commonly bought dollars to protect their savings. I asked Neyla who the other passengers were and she pointed to two men coming down the path. The forestry agents. I groaned audibly and Neyla laughed. "At least we're getting rid of them," she whispered. That afternoon I was back in Trinidad still surprised that I had pulled it off. I had left the city only four days earlier.

The following morning I went looking for Jack Anderson. As Silva had predicted, I had no trouble locating the church which was only a couple of blocks from the hotel. There was no one inside so I walked around to the back. Behind the church was a one-room house built up against a back wall. There were people inside cooking and talking. A man came out to greet me, and I was invited inside the house and introduced to the others. They were Sirionó, I was told, who had come in from Ibiato. One of the women had burned her face with hot lard and had needed medical attention. She stepped forward so I could see her injury. The grease had blistered her face but she appeared to be healing well. I asked them where I might find Juanito, and they gave me directions to a house on the outskirts of the city.

Another strike was on to protest some new governmental decree so I couldn't find a "moto-taxi" (motorcycles that serve as taxis). I walked about two kilometers until I found the house that had been described to me. A young mestizo maid let me in the front gate, explaining that the Andersons had gone shopping. They should be back soon, she said, so I could wait. Twenty minutes later, a Land Rover pulled up and an older couple climbed out.

Jack Anderson was not a large man; he was on the thin side and walked with a slight stoop. There was a remarkable resemblance between Anderson and the old Austrian priest, Fr. Hildebert. Both were of small stature, fair-skinned with strong, craggy features, and both had a beautiful shock of full, white hair. Jack's wife, Darlene, was his physical opposite: a large, heavyset woman with a generous laugh.

I introduced myself and told the Andersons of my interest in the Sirionó. I also decided to let them know that I was an anthropologist. In the past this revelation had brought different responses, ranging from wary evasiveness to open hostility. I was braced for their reaction, but none came. As we talked, I was also relieved at not being asked about my religious beliefs, something I had come to expect from fundamentalists. The Andersons were proving not only tolerable but enjoyable. As Jack related stories about his life with the Sirionó, I had the impression that he wanted to be back in Ibiato, not there in Trinidad and that the Sirionó were the only people he felt comfortable with. When I asked why he had left Ibiato, the village he built, to come to Trinidad twenty years ago, there was an unmistakable sadness in his reply. His mother had died, leaving the church in Trinidad unattended; and his wife had tired of living in the wilderness.

Jack then told me something of his past. He was born in Los Angeles in 1917. His father, Thomas, was the son of missionaries who had worked in China where a man named Dan Crawford told him about the Indians in Bolivia. In 1920, the elder Anderson packed up his family and went to La Paz in hopes of finding missionary work in the Bolivian lowlands. A revolution interfered with his plans and the family spent five years in the highland community of Punata.

When Jack's parents returned to Los Angeles, they became involved in a new Pentecostal movement called Four Square Gospel headed by Aimee Semple McPherson, who built the Angelus Temple in Los Angeles, a spectacular monument to faith and affluence. Their doctrine was fundamental Christianity but with the glitter of southern California of the late 1920s. Jack showed me a large publicity photo of Aimee McPherson, and I was surprised to see not a stern-faced, drab apostle of Christianity but a beautiful woman in a satin gown sitting at a white piano. Her hair was done in the crisp style of the twenties and her face elegantly made up. Emblazoned on her chest was a sequined cross. In 1929, Thomas Anderson and his wife returned to

Bolivia, this time to Trinidad, as Four Square missionaries. Mrs. Anderson, following the example of her leader, wore makeup and earrings. The other missionary wives were horrified. Protestant missionaries overseas, even those from disparate sects, form a tightly knit, clannish group that will not tolerate deviance. When Jack's mother refused to remove her makeup and earrings, she was ostracized. Thus Jack grew up in circumstances unknown among missionary families: he spent virtually no time around other missionaries and their children. He did not attend a missionary boarding school. He received only rudimentary education in the field, growing up among the Indians. His lack of "proper training" led to unconventional behavior that only widened the gap between his family and much of the mission community.

Jack's father established his first Sirionó mission at a ranch about six leagues (30 kilometers) beyond Ibiato. There was a small group of Sirionó working for the rancher there in exchange for safety from the Ayoreo. Thomas then contacted another group and decided to set up a place for the Indians where they would not be subject to a rancher's demands. The Sirionó told him about Ibiato, the land-hump, where the ground was high and cool breezes blew. Thomas took his sons, Jack, twelve, and Paul, twenty, to survey the site. Finding it to his liking, Thomas left the two boys in charge of the Indians while he returned to Trinidad. Jack and Paul set to work with the Sirionó clearing land and building houses. Their father never returned permanently to Ibiato, remaining instead in Trinidad to establish a church there, evidently at the behest of the Four Square governing committee. After two years, Paul tired of life in the wilderness, never really liking the long, hard expeditions in search of more Indians. At the age of fourteen, Jack made his first trip accompanied only by a few Sirionó men and successfully contacted an unacculturated band. Paul eventually left Ibiato, and Jack continued alone the work of settling Sirionó at the mission.

From all accounts—Concha's, Silva's, the Sirionós, and Jack's—it would appear that life for the Indians at Ibiato was probably not much different from that at Casarabe. Jack, like everyone else of that era, equated "civilization" with hard work. There was a six-day work week: three for the mission to pay for the school and a teacher as well as other expenses, and three for each Sirionó to clear and work his own farmland. Jack claimed he never condoned the severe beating of Indians although the Sirionó caciques commonly used whipping (learned from local mestizos) as a form of punishment for such behavior as laziness, fighting, or stealing. On rare occasions the Sirionó at Ibiato would bring alcohol into the village; if discovered, they were flogged. As the numbers of Sirionó at Ibiato grew, Jack hired mestizos, presumably well-recommended, to help oversee the work teams. A cattle herd had been started, which also required additional labor. According to Jack, the mestizos rarely could be trusted and there was frequent turnover in personnel because of mistreatment of Indians.

I asked Jack about Allan Holmberg. He remembered him only vaguely, saying that Holmberg had come to Ibiato once and Jack had seen him a few times in Casarabe. Because of the hatred between Anderson and Loayza, it would be unlikely that Holmberg would have risked the wrath of the camp director to strike up a friendship with the missionary. I also suspect that Holmberg tended to view Ibiato as just another "Indian camp" where he could learn no more than what he had at Casarabe.

Jack lived alone in Ibiato with the Sirionó until he was almost thirty. During that time, a great many Indians died from diseases which he did not have the expertise nor medication to treat. In addition to his work at the mission, he began to acquire wilderness land to build his own cattle herd, a move that brought further criticism from the missionary community. Jack was vehement in his defense of this move: he wanted freedom from total dependence on mission support for his work.

Shortly before his thirtieth birthday, and no doubt at his mother's urging, Jack returned to California to find a wife. In Los Angeles, he met the daughter of an American missionary working in South Africa, and they were married within the year. Darlene Anderson, a trained nurse, returned with Jack to Ibiato. They lived there until about 1964, when Jack's mother died and the Andersons and their four sons moved to Trinidad. Jack took up the work his mother had left and continues to preach in the old downtown Four Square Gospel church.

Jack and I talked into the late afternoon, and I was invited to dinner so that we could continue. Like Silva, Jack spoke of the early expeditions to find Sirionó. He also talked of the post-revolution years when he finally received permission from the authorities in Trinidad to remove Sirionó from local ranches, regardless of debts incurred, and bring them to Ibiato.

It was during these forays to locate Sirionó that Anderson "confiscated" the Indians Silva had contacted. Whenever word reached Jack that a group of Sirionó had been settled on a farm or ranch, Jack would form a "comission" of men from Ibiato and go after them. In most instances, government documents would suffice to free the Indians from someone's land; but now and then, a rancher would protest and Jack would have to draw his gun and threaten force. Fortunately, he said, there was never any bloodshed.

As the evening drew to a close, I told the Andersons that I wanted to try to get to Ibiato the next day. Jack said that there was a new road which passed by Casarabe and ultimately would go through to Santa Cruz but that it was still unsurfaced. Since the weather had been dry he thought I could probably find a truck going that way. Before I left, he would send a message by public radio to Ibiato so someone could meet me with horses in Casarabe.

The Andersons invited me for breakfast the next morning so we could work out the details of the trip.

When I left the hotel the following day, there still were no moto-taxis and the city seemed even quieter. I walked out to the Anderson place. Darlene told me that the Comité Cívica (Civic Committee) had declared a citywide strike and that no vehicles were being allowed in or out. By sealing off Trinidad and inconveniencing everyone for a few days, they would bring the government in La Paz to its knees. I didn't understand the logic, but Bolivian politics, especially in the lowlands, are often a mystery even to the natives.

My concern now was that I had only ten days left. I had to find a way to Ibiato. I told Jack that I had some official-looking documents from my university and the National Museum of Bolivia authorizing my work there. If I could get to the right people, those papers might allow me to travel. Jack said he knew several of the men on the Comité, including the president.

Impressed by all the stamps, seals, and ribbons on my papers, the president of the Comité Cívica gave me a pass to leave the city. We found a moto-taxi driver who had a big Suzuki dirt bike that looked as though it would make the 70-kilometer trip. The driver was skeptical that we would get through the roadblock and really didn't want to go all the way out to Casarabe. He wasn't even certain where Ibiato was. I offered him U.S. $10, the equivalent of about two days' wages, and he agreed.

We were both surprised to get through the blockade with my pass. The trip was long and dusty, and the knapsack bouncing on my back made my shoulders ache. We had lunch at a little town, then it was back to the pounding of the road. At about 3 p.m. we arrived in Casarabe. It had by now attained mythical proportions in my mind, but it was just another town with a ragged plaza and some adobe houses. Whatever might have remained of Holmberg's days had been erased by time. Most of the people living there had no idea of Casarabe's origins. It was a mestizo town through and through. The Sirionó were long gone.

After a cold soda at one of Casarabe's several drinking establishments, we asked directions to Ibiato. We were shown a trail leading north out of town. It was ten kilometers, we were told. I was puzzled because everything I had read and heard indicated that Ibiato was just five kilometers from Casarabe. It was explained that a new road was being cut toward El Carmen and passed within three kilometers of Ibiato but that it took a roundabout route. The shorter route was through marshland and could only be made by horse or riding ox. The road was high and dry. After about six or seven kilometers, we crossed a wood and earth bridge and then saw a wide, well-used trail leading off into the woods. We followed it to an open area that looked like the old airstrip Jack had told me about. The pigs had rooted up large areas of the ground, making it unusable. We made a dogleg turn to the right and there it was, one of the strangest sights I have seen.

I had known Ibiato was located on a Mojos Indian mound; but since this was my first trip to the Beni, I had never actually seen one before. I wasn't expecting much more than a small hump of land; what confronted me was a huge, three-level mound that rose at least 35 to 40 feet in the air. At the top, literally on the mound's pinnacle, stood the church Jack had built thirty years earlier. It was constructed of adobe and Spanish tile, but the design was right out of middle America. On the next two levels were thatched houses and a few with tile roofs. When we rode up to the second level, I could see a large, square, tile-roofed house behind the church. That would be the Anderson home, now a virtual ruin with only the roof and walls remaining. The noise of the motorcycle brought people running from their homes. They had been expecting us since receiving Jack's message on Radio Trópico at noon. I paid the moto-taxi driver and he sped off, wanting to be in Casarabe before dark. I had a note from Jack addressed to the town's pastor, Chiro Cuellar, asking him to find lodging for me. Chiro stepped forward, a tall, handsome Sirionó I judged to be in his mid-thirties. He welcomed me to Ibiato and then invited me to his house for something to drink. The crowd followed. I met his wife, Nancy, and his eldest son, William. All of the Sirionó houses were small. Chiro's was larger than most but consisted of only one room. There were three beds for Chiro, Nancy, and their six children. Two were wooden planks laid across supports set in the earthen floor. The third was in the style of lowland furniture of years past: a cowhide nailed over a wooden frame. A table with two benches occupied the center of the house. We were seated at the table with what seemed to be most of the village pressed around us. I told them who I was and something of the places I had visited. They were eager to hear about the people in Salvatierra and especially those in San Pedro. I told them I had been with Jêjê and that he was well. There were murmurs of pleasure and approval. Almost tentatively, I broached the subject of my interest: the Sirionó people themselves. There was no hesitancy at all. These people proudly referred to themselves as Sirionó and eagerly responded to my questions. They wanted *me* to know about *them*.

When it got dark, Chiro told me I could stay in the house Perry and Anne Priest had built when they were working on Bible translation and would stay in Ibiato. Jack hadn't said much about Perry so I hadn't been able to determine the nature of their relationship. I knew only that when Jack and Darlene left Ibiato, Perry and Anne Priest moved there from San Pedro. Unlike the Andersons, the Priests did not live permanently in Ibiato, but worked out of their mission headquarters in Tumi Chuqua.

The Priest house was rustic and in need of repair, but it had a roof and offered a little privacy. It also had the only outhouse in town. It was a long night. There was a bed of wood planks and no mattress. I dozed in snatches, then would have to find a more comfortable position. To add to my problem, the house was surrounded by cows. Ibiato's cattle evidently had chosen that particular site for the night. I discovered that cows do not sleep; they urinate, defecate, and chew their cuds almost without respite. By 4 a.m. or so, exhaustion took over and I finally slept. I was surprised when I awoke that it was already 7 a.m. The village was only beginning to stir. Throughout my stay, I marveled at the late waking hours of the Sirionó. In every other instance of my experience among rural lowlanders, the day began at dawn. While it was common for Sirionó men going on a hunt to leave early, perhaps even in the middle of the night, those remaining in the village approached the new day with relative indifference. There was really no need to rise early, especially if it were cold or raining.

I took my meals with Chiro and Nancy, who were the most acculturated of the Sirionó and therefore the most at ease with an outsider. Nancy assumed the role of guide and informant. We visited a few of the homes and talked with the residents. It was all very formal, and I probably felt almost as uncomfortable as they did. Nancy explained that everyone in the village was either Sirionó or married to one. I asked her how many non-Sirionó lived there and she said four or five at the most. She had no idea of the total population, telling me that some of the people, particularly the older Sirionó, lived in their chacos about 10 kilometers away. Later, I asked Chiro the same question. He told me that he thought there were about 250 people in Ibiato and the surrounding area. He also explained that no one was allowed on Sirionó land who was not Sirionó or married to one.

"What happens if a man cohabits with a Sirionó woman, and they split up. Can he stay here?" I asked.

"Only if he takes another Sirionó woman. If he does not, or leaves to being in another woman from the outside, the ererucas will tell him to leave."

I was impressed. At last, a sense of group solidarity and ethnic consciousness. Then I knew I had to ask the unavoidable follow-up question: "How did this all start?"

"Juanito feels it is best this way. And he is right. If we let others in, they would take all our land and before we knew it, we would have nothing."

I suppose I knew the answer all along, that Jack, not the Indians, had made this rule. What was fascinating was not so much his past influence on Ibiato but the fact that after twenty years' absence from the community his involvement with Ibiato's affairs was so evident. Chiro then told me that Jack came out to Ibiato two or three times a year; and of course when Sirionó went to Trinidad, they could stay at the church without cost. Still, given the fact that Jack no longer lived there, it was remarkable that the intensity of the relationship between Anderson and Ibiato had remained so strong.

I enjoyed my stay in Ibiato and being around Sirionó who were not ashamed of their origins and enjoyed talking about their past. I was relieved to discover that places like Salvatierra and San Pedro were not all that was left of these people. As a result of all my travels and conversations I had determined that there were no other Sirionó communities to be found. Ibiato was the Sirionó's last stand.

The Sunday following my arrival, a man from the Public Health Department arrived in a pickup truck to give DPT shots to the children. He was a mestizo and a member of Jack's church in Trinidad who had donated his day off to visit Ibiato. Since my time was now very short, I had to make use of the available transportation back to Trinidad. I said goodbye to the villagers and thanked Chiro and Nancy for their help. I told Nancy that if things worked out, I would probably be back in a year to spend several months in Ibiato. I had made up my mind: though by default, Ibiato would be the site of my restudy of the Sirionó.

"Nancy"

*Part
Two*

SIX
Chapter 6

When I returned from Bolivia at the end of the summer of 1982, I applied for and was granted a sabbatical leave for the following academic year. During the interim, I began to formulate more precisely my research objectives for returning to Ibiato. At the outset, I knew that I did not want to attempt the "classic" type of restudy, or one in which the researcher reevaluates the validity of the original investigator's work. I had serious reservations about such projects, which always produced debatable results. In 1926–27, for example, Robert Redfield studied the Mexican peasant community of Tepoztlán, describing the village and its inhabitants in somewhat idyllic terms. Seventeen years later, Oscar Lewis visited Tepoztlán only to discover a very different situation. The people he studied could be malicious, spiteful, greedy, and grasping. Whose view was correct? Or, as some suspected, had the intervening years simply changed what Redfield had first reported?

The most controversial case of a restudy is that involving Derek Freeman and Margaret Mead. Freeman's argument that Mead's Samoan data were faulty gained worldwide attention not only because of Mead's eminence but also because she no longer was around to defend herself, compelling others to take up her banner. In both cases, Mexico and Samoa, a significant amount of time elapsed between the original and the follow-up research, and so many new variables had been introduced that the comparisons were virtually meaningless.

I believe that the value of a restudy is not in trying to replicate findings (as a chemist who can satisfactorily perform an identical experiment twenty years later) but in assessing the changes that have occurred since the original study. Mead herself returned to several field sites for this purpose as have many anthropologists involved in long-term research on social change. Nonetheless, the availability of earlier research, whatever its shortcomings, is of inestimable value. As Theodore Schwartz explained, trying to understand and evaluate change without such baseline data would be "like studying embryology from scrambled eggs."

My interest in restudying the Sirionó, then, was not to challenge Allan Holmberg's results. Since more than forty years had passed between Holmberg's research and my own, the notion bordered on the absurd. Interviews I had conducted in Bolivia with elderly Sirionó and "old hands" like Silva and Anderson convinced me that, by and large, Holmberg's ethnography was an accurate portrayal of unacculturated and recently acculturated Sirionó of that time. It provided me with a more than adequate cultural panorama with which present-day Sirionó society could be compared and contrasted.

My trip to Bolivia in search of the Sirionó had also reinforced my earlier sentiments on the need for a restudy focusing on current issues, one that was necessary not only from an academic standpoint but from that of the Sirionó themselves. Publications in their own country and abroad that purported to present recent findings but pictured the Sirionó walking nude through the forest carrying bows and arrows are understandably a source of concern. They consider themselves part of modern society and are anxious for the world to accept them as such.

Also as a result of my preliminary fieldwork, I realized that the cultural survival of the Sirionó at Ibiato was an important topic for consideration. By all standards, the Sirionó, like so many other small groups of foragers before them, should have disappeared. I observed this process under way in places like Salvatierra and along the Río Blanco where, in another fifteen or twenty years, the last vestiges of their culture will be gone. But Ibiato had survived despite the odds against it and despite Holmberg's prediction of failure. I was convinced that the reasons for this persistence were worth discovering. Thus, my primary research objectives were two: to provide a description of modern-day Sirionó to place them in the context of a larger society and to determine what factors had contributed to Ibiato's survival.

Arriving at these objectives had been easy: they were predetermined by existing circumstances. In this case, the realities of the field situation had formulated the problem—I had not devised the problem beforehand and then gone looking for a place to study it. What caused greater indecision and introspection was the issue of dealing with Ibiato as a fundamentalist Protestant mission. In my experience, anthropologists either ignore the missionary presence, perhaps mentioning it briefly in an introduction to their ethnography before getting on with more important matters, or they reserve their remarks for publications focusing on missionaries as a special topic, such as David Stoll's *Fishers of Men or Founders of Empire?* and Hvalkof and Aaby's *Is God an American?* My first inclination was to take the former course. For a while, I tried to convince myself that I had satisfied my research obligations in piecing together Ibiato's history by talking to Jack Anderson and now that he no longer resided in the village, I, too, could get on with the business at hand. That would be the end of missionary presence in my work. But ultimately I had to face the fact that Ibiato was Anderson's creation and even though he might not be physically present in the community, he and the Sirionó were inextricably bound together. Then too, there was the inescapable fact that Ibiato was the survivor, not Casarabe or Tibaera or Las Piedras, not Santa María or Salvatierra, and that this fact must be linked in some way to the old missionary. Finally, there was the matter of the other missionary, Perry Priest; I knew he had a part in the story as well. Dealing with missionaries from a value-free perspective, simply as elements in the process of social change and adaptation, was an idea I was not comfortable with. But if I were going to understand the nature of this survival, I would have to attempt to study the missionary presence as dispassionately and objectively as I would my primary subjects, the Sirionó.

I had to take my sabbatical leave from September through April, ideal months for someone working in temperate climates north of the equator, but for eastern Bolivia, the timing couldn't have been worse. Most of my stay would fall in the midst of the rainy season which could make any form of travel impossible for weeks at a time. In anticipation of this, I made a decision that, in view of my twenty years' experience in this region, was embarrassingly ill advised.

In addition to my proposed Sirionó restudy, I wanted to spend some time with the Yuquí, a recently contacted band of foragers culturally related to the Sirionó. Because they lived in a much more remote area, I decided to visit them first, taking advantage of the end of the dry season. What I hadn't taken into account was that the Yuquí could be reached by air year around. The New Tribes missionaries who had contacted this group had built an excellent airstrip to support their work. On the other hand, Ibiato, which I had thought would be easier to reach because of its proximity to Trinidad, turned out to be virtually inaccessible in bad weather. The road I had traveled over for my previous dry-season visit had made the 70-kilometer trip seem deceptively easy. Later, that same road would become impassable, with long stretches under water more than a meter deep.

I returned to Bolivia on September 1, 1983, and spent just four months, or half my sabbatical, with the Yuquí as planned. When I came out, I flew to Trinidad to try to arrange for housing in Ibiato. The weather was holding, and trucks were continuing to make trips to Casarabe and beyond. I met with Jack Anderson, who suggested I stay in his old house. There were always one or two Sirionó families staying there temporarily, he said, but he thought I could find an empty room, fix it up a bit, and be quite comfortable. The house was in bad shape, Jack admitted, but the roof was still sound. The place belonging to Perry Priest, where I had stayed during my initial visit, would not do on a long-term basis. The Priests were known to show up from time to time and would need their house. I also had considered building my own quarters; but after just having gone through that experience among the Yuquí where I had no choice, I was not eager to try it again so soon. Since time was also a major consideration, I felt that any available structure that offered some work space and privacy would be preferable to building a house from scratch.

Jack told me he would be going to Ibiato in a week or two, if the weather remained favorable, and offered to find a room for me in the old house and see what needed to be done to make it livable. I left him U.S. $50 to cover any materials and labor and then flew to Santa Cruz for Christmas with friends and a needed rest.

The rainy season arrived with a vengeance in the new year. Radio broadcasts and newspapers were filled with reports of devastation in the Beni. Rivers had overflowed their banks, leaving scores of people homeless. Thousands of cattle had drowned or starved to death and many more were in danger of dying from standing continually in water up to their bellies.

Against the advice my friends, I flew to Trinidad with all my gear, determined to get to Ibiato. As the plane descended, my heart sank. The city looked like an island in the middle of an enormous lake. Sandbags were piled in strategic points to keep the floodwaters at bay. I could see a long stretch of the Casarabe road, most of it under water. The prospect of having to return to Santa Cruz to wait out the remainder of the rainy season was devastating—I might as well go home. My sense of defeat heightened when I got to the hotel where I normally stayed. It was full, and so was the next and the next. People were stranded in the city, particularly the itinerant merchants and the newer crowd, the cocaine traffickers who worked the outlying areas. In desperation, I arranged for one hotel to keep an eye on my numerous sacks of gear and supplies while I walked out to the Andersons to see if they could suggest something. They insisted that I stay with them. At first I hesitated. Although they appeared more open-minded than other fundamentalist missionaries I had known, I was by now wary of being subjected to the proselytizing I had experienced with fundamentalists while among the Yuquí. Given the circumstances, I had few alternatives. If I had to remain in Trinidad for an indeterminate period, at least I could use the time productively by talking with Jack about Ibiato and the Sirionó. More than a year had passed since that first brief visit, and I had a great many more questions. My fears of the Andersons' religious fervor were unfounded, however, and I was welcomed into their home simply as a guest.

Jack sensed my anxiety over the delay and tried to console me by explaining that if there were three or four days of hot, dry weather, I could probably get through. He then laughed and said if I wanted, I could go by ox cart, which would mean about a week or ten days of slogging through the mud. I failed to see the humor since I knew this might end up being my only option.

As if on command, the weather turned hot and dry and the water began to recede. The road west opened for transport, but the road east to Casarabe remained impassable. I waited a few days more and then went looking for a truck to hire. No one wanted to try it. Several truck owners told me that the big state-owned farm tractor with a trailer would be going out to carry passengers and supplies but that it was being repaired. No one could give me any assurances of a departure date. Finally, I found a man who needed the money badly enough to risk the trip. His truck was incredibly beat up, an old Toyota with no bumpers or fenders and only one headlight. The truck bed sat at a very strange angle and there was no reverse gear (which, the driver assured me, was nothing to worry about since we would only be going forward). Worst of all, the truck had no four-wheel drive, an absolute necessity for lowland travel. I wondered how many days we would sit stranded in the middle of the Beni.

We started out early the next morning with a few passengers, mostly men, to help weigh down the rear wheels for traction and to push when necessary. The driver also brought along his younger brother, Pablo, who looked like a Bolivian version of the Incredible Hulk. I stopped counting how many times we got stuck after the first three hours. We dug and pushed and dug some more. A huge hemp rope was finally tied around the front end of the truck and while the rest of us pushed from the rear, Pablo hauled on the rope, almost single-handedly pulling us through much of the quagmire. The passengers and I cheered him on, bringing forth astounding efforts and a huge grin. One of the men told me Pablo was famous in Trinidad for his feats of strength and could lift up the whole front end of the truck if he had to. I believed him.

At 3:30 that afternoon we pulled into Casarabe. It had taken eight and a half hours to travel 59 kilometers. The Sirionó, having received Jack's public radio message, were there waiting with horses. I thanked the trucker, gave him a bonus, and we loaded up the horses for the ten kilometer ride to Ibiato. At the wooden bridge, we stopped at a house to pick up a woman and her infant daughter. The baby was very sick, with a fever and chest congestion, and her mother wanted to get her to Ibiato where she could obtain antibiotics.

Nancy, Chiro, and most of the townspeople were out to greet us as we rode up the hill to the small plaza opposite the church. Chiro led my horse to the side of the Anderson house where he told me a room had been made ready. Nancy gave me a hug and the kids swarmed around to have a better look at this newest "Abae" (white person) who would live among them.

My first impressions of the Anderson house the year before had been largely correct. On that earlier trip I had looked in briefly but was discouraged from further exploration by the huge numbers of bats living up under the roof. At that time the place seemed dark, dirty, in ruins, and just plain spooky. Now, as dusk settled over Ibiato, it looked even worse. The room I would occupy was at the front of the house which faced away from the village, looking west toward Trinidad. It was a large room with a semicircular front wall in which stood five large openings that at one time had been windows. With the money I had left him, Jack had had these screened. They would become the saving grace of my graceless abode, giving me a panoramic view from the top of the mound of the forest and plains beyond. The remainder of the room consisted of the skeleton of what once had been a built-in cabinet of shelves and drawers, scarred and blackened adobe walls, and a brick floor covered with hardened patches of clay deposited by children and animals who trekked through the house. The floor had been swept and an old door hung on a warped frame. Edilberto Yoseté, an older Sirionó who occupied the room behind mine with his wife and her son, had woven some palm fronds into large mats which were nailed to the rafters. These formed a ceiling of sorts to help control the bats. The bats, however, had already discovered how to crawl through the spaces in the weaving, and several were flitting about the room. No one seemed to notice them, so I tried to ignore them as well.

The villagers were warm in their welcome and eagerly set to making my room more comfortable. There seemed to be agreement that Abae need more "things." A table was brought with a chair. Two small school desks were also provided for my books and papers. A real bed appeared from someone's house, evidently a leftover from the defunct clinic. It was just a wooden planked affair, but I had a cotton mattress and a small piece of foam rubber which made it quite comfortable. I unpacked by duffel bag and placed my clothing on the table in neat piles. Everyone enjoyed watching all this. One of the children took my bucket and filled it with water for drinking and washing. I made up my bed, strung my mosquito net, and was moved in. Nancy invited me to their house for supper—*masaco* (a lowland staple of mashed cooked plantains, lard, and salt) and one of my favorites that she had remembered from the previous year, *paja cedrón* (lemon grass) tea. During supper we discussed my taking *pensión*, meals, with them for 2,000 pesos, or about U.S. 90 cents a day. It would mean extra income for the family, would free me from the time-consuming task of finding and preparing food, and would give me an excuse to be a continual presence in their home.

It was dark when I returned to my room. As I walked through what had once been the living room to cross to my door, I almost ran into a large cow. I had my flashlight on and it wasn't that I couldn't see the cow, I just wasn't expecting one. *"Fuera!"* I yelled. "Out!" Edilberto heard me shout and, grabbing a stick, chased the cow outside. "We have to do something about this," he said. "The animals are always coming in here and making messes all over the floor. Tomorrow I am going to put a fence in front of the door." He did as he promised, and for the remainder of my stay in Ibiato I entered the house by climbing through a window.

But there was more to come. When I opened the door to my room, I froze in the doorway. Roaches and spiders scurried up and down the walls and the air was thick with bats; but the pièce de résistance was a knot of huge toads huddled together on the floor staring at me with glassy, yellow eyes. I grabbed the broom that fortunately was standing by the door and flailed at everything in sight. When the wildlife retreated enough for me to make my way to my bed, I crawled in under the net and pulled the covers over my head.

When morning came at last, Nancy's children eagerly set to work catching the toads by a hind foot and lobbing them out the door. In the meantime, I strung up over my bed a large plastic tarp to cut down on both the bats and their refuse which had sifted down on me all night. Then we walked over to Nancy's for breakfast. She was visibly upset. The baby we had brought with us the day before had died during the night. Then Nancy told me that the baby's mother had purchased some antibiotics from one of the villagers and that she, Nancy, had agreed to give the injection free of charge. But when she went to the house to administer the antibiotics, there was a *bruja* (sorceress) working on the failing infant. Nancy explained that a new family had arrived from Salvatierra just a few days earlier. One of the women, a Sirionó, had been married to a Guarayo *brujo* and evidently had learned some of his skills. While I was in Salvatierra, Concha had surreptitiously pointed out a powerful brujo named Clemente. Witchcraft is prevalent among the Guarayo, whose expertise in it is widely known and feared in eastern Bolivia. This was the first indication I had that the Guarayo influence had permeated Ibiato as well.

The woman from Salvatierra had gone to visit the sick child and had convinced the mother that, for a fee, she would "suck out" the foreign objects in the child's body that some enemy of the mother had supposedly put there. The bruja placed her mouth over the baby and extracted several thorns and nails by "sucking" them out. The mother and others present were awed by her performance. Hours later, the baby died. The bruja claimed that the evil was so strong that she had not been able to extract it all. When Nancy asked me what I thought, I told her that it was an old trick, that the objects were placed in the mouth by sleight of hand and then would miraculously appear as if "sucked" out of the child. (I was tempted to borrow an egg and show her how I could make it appear to come out of someone's ear but decided that if word got around, I, too, would probably be labeled a witch.) Nancy seemed to accept my explanation but remained uncertain and afraid. Chiro was adamant that the woman should cease her activities. Every time there was someone like this in Ibiato, he said, bad things happened and everyone began to suspect everyone else of having evil spells cast, or practicing *hechicería*.

The infant was buried that same afternoon giving me a sad and abrupt introduction to the ritual behavior of the Sirionó at Ibiato. Nonetheless, I was curious to see how closely Ibiato's burial customs resembled those of other lowland communities, albeit Catholic. Since the Sirionó had no indigenous tradition of burial, instead abandoning the dead in the forest, I knew that the ritual I was about to observe would be the result of acculturation: the Sirionó interpretation of American and European customs of Christian burial.

In general, the funeral differed little from the many I have attended in rural Santa Cruz. An effort to make some type of coffin produced a crude box consisting of a few nailed boards of uneven length. The top was a flattened piece of cardboard from a carton of powdered milk which bore the words "Donated by the People of the United States of America." It was tied on with a vine. As is customary when a child dies, the coffin was carried by children down to the graveyard at the edge of the old airstrip. A hole already dug, was too small and had to be widened, and then two men lowered the box into the pit. Vicente, one of the Sirionó pastors, read from the Bible, a hymn was sung, and the grave was covered. It all struck me as fairly routine until I looked around. We were standing in the middle of the woods. There was no visible sign that anyone else had been buried in the area. Although people in the lowlands are not known for keeping their cemeteries well tended, once a year, on the eve of All Souls' Day, they visit the graves of deceased relatives and clean out the weeds. The remainder of the year the place is ignored, except for burials, when an area is cleared away for the occasion. Still, even in an overgrown state, there is no mistaking that a cemetery is there. We were standing among full-grown trees. There were no grave markers or other signs that this was a burial ground. I leaned over and asked Vicente, "Where is everybody?" As soon as I had spoken, I realized my question was a little peculiar. But Vicente understood: "Oh, they're all in here." He lifted his right arm and pointed to various places, telling me who was buried where. Then he commented that they really should think about cleaning the place out sometime. Because Ibiato is a Protestant community which does not observe All Souls' Day, there is no specific time set aside to do this, so it doesn't get done. But I also had the feeling that Vicente was responding to what he felt was my concern, not his own. I suspect the Sirionó are perfectly at ease with the idea that one of their own is buried in an unmarked grave in the midst of the woods. In the past, the dead were left behind with only the skull recovered perhaps at some later time to be carried with the group on its wanderings. Eventually, the skull as well would be abandoned. Now, the dead were comfortably gathered in one place, in the midst of the forest where they belonged, and grave markers were an unnecessary clutter.

When we left the cemetery the sun was droping behind the church. My first day in Ibiato was ending. The next four months would bring new discoveries and experiences as well as days of interminable boredom. Life in Ibiato moved at its own pace and was not to be rushed.

"The Church Ibiato"

SEVEN

Chapter 7

After my first month in Ibiato, I began to feel more a part of village life. During those first weeks I completed a census, something the villagers were familiar with from radio broadcasts, although the National Census Bureau had never actually visited the town. It gave me the opportunity to talk to various members of every household and thus speed up the process of getting to know as many people as possible. Nancy accompanied me when I visited the outlying areas, helping me locate isolated farmsteads that I otherwise would have missed. For her, it was a rare opportunity to delegate her household chores to others and have a few days to exchange news and gossip with neighbors she saw only infrequently.

While in the process of going house to house, I also mapped the town, locating each structure in relation to others on and around the mound (see Fig. 3). Evidently this had never been done before; it created interest and curiosity among the residents when they saw their houses visually depicted on a large sheet of paper I carried with me. Our final tally was 267 inhabitants including both Ibiato proper and its surrounding areas. The male-female ratio was 138 to 129, but six of the males were non-Sirionó, bringing the Sirionó male-female ratio to 132/129. I wondered why there were no outside females married to Sirionó men and, when I asked several of the villagers, got much the same answer: mestizo men are attracted to Sirionó women because they make "good wives," i.e., they are quiet, loving, submissive, and thrifty. Mestizo women, on the other hand, were characterized as domineering, abrasive, loud, and untrustworthy. In my own experience with mestizo

Figure 3

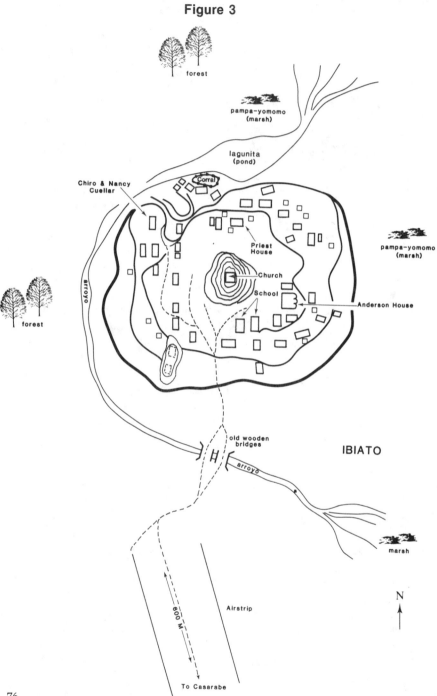

forest

pampa-yomomo
(marsh)

lagunita
(pond)

Chiro & Nancy
Cuellar

Corral

Priest
House

pampa-yomomo
(marsh)

arroyo

forest

Church

School

Anderson House

old wooden
bridges

IBIATO

arroyo

marsh

N

Airstrip

600 M.

To Casarabe

women of lowland Bolivia, I have found them to be quite independent and some even aggressive, especially when compared to most Sirionó women. Nonetheless, I encountered several Sirionó women in Ibiato who were very forthright and outspoken in making their opinions known. After a while, I realized that this stereotyping of mestizo and Sirionó women was perpetuated by the telling and retelling of the same stories I had heard. Even young boys would scowl and frown if I teased them about marrying a non-Sirionó woman. The adolescent girls giggled at the prospect of marrying a mestizo man. In these discussions, both serious and playful, it became apparent that there were other influences as well on the selection of a spouse. Jack Anderson and Perry Priest had actively lobbied against the marrying of non-Sirionó. Chiro explained that both missionaries saw it as a potential threat to the integrity of the town, the continuation of the Sirionó as a people, the sanctity of their land, and, of course, the preservation of their Protestant faith.

Another interesting bit of data to emerge from the census was the age distribution of Ibiato's residents. When I plotted a population pyramid, the result was an hourglass configuration (see Fig. 4). Typically, this type of pyramid is indicative of out-migration. I had suspected that some working-age Sirionó were leaving the community to seek their fortunes elsewhere. My suspicions were confirmed by several informants who told of grown children, brothers, or sisters who had moved away. I expect this trend to continue, especially since transportation routes are improving and communication is becoming more sophisticated, exposing the Sirionó to even greater temptations to leave Ibiato and explore the world outside.

Although I knew that young adult Sirionó had left the community, other census data presented an alternative explanation for the particular configuration of Ibiato's population. My interviews with older Sirionó revealed that most had lost significant numbers of children (two women had lost all their children, a total of eighteen infants) as a result of the various epidemics that spread through Ibiato during the 1940s and 1950s. Had those offspring lived, most would fall into the 30-40-year-old age cohorts where the population now has its smallest numbers. If disease has in fact had more impact on the mid-range population than has migration, then Ibiato may actually experience some growth as the younger Sirionó reach childbearing age. This more optimistic picture of Ibiato's future may be helped by in-migration to the village. Recently, economic hardship in Bolivia has encouraged Sirionó located along the Río Blanco and in the Guarayo region to seek refuge in Ibiato. During just the relatively short time I was there, four new families moved into Ibiato. According to village tradition, as long as a prospective resident can establish Sirionó ties through blood or marriage, he or she is welcomed into the community and given land to farm.

One of these more recent arrivals was Marta Moreno and her twelve-

Figure 4

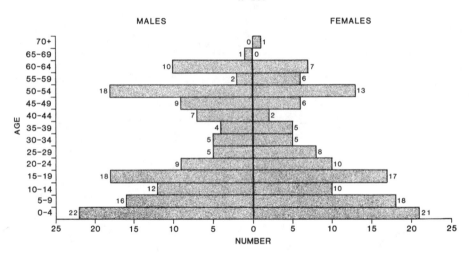

POPULATION OF IBIATO
1984
N=267

year-old son, René, who were now living with the other occupant of my house, Edilberto Yoseté. Marta was born in Ibiato but at about age five went with her parents to the Franciscan mission of Santa María, near Salvatierra. Later, she traveled up the Río Blanco to El Carmen where she cohabited with a Sirionó raised by mestizos there, Nicolás Antelo. When he died, Marta decided to return to her birthplace. She struck up a friendship with Edilberto, at that time without a spouse, and moved in with him.

In talking with Ibiato's residents, I found that many had similar stories. They had traveled around a great deal during the early years of contact, escaping from one ranch only to be indentured on another and moving from mission to pacification camp to mission as stories spread of better or worse living conditions in these places. Several Sirionó I talked to evidently went through a period of "shopping around," looking for a place to settle. They were also, no doubt, experiencing the discomfort of knowing that their old nomadic way of life was coming to an end but were prolonging the inevitable for as long as possible.

Marta, like most of her contemporaries, knew the whereabouts of other Sirionó, perhaps not specific locations or individuals, but a sense of which families had settled where. Thus, newcomers to Ibiato had little trouble in identifying themselves simply by reciting names of various relatives. Invariably, some near relative would be related to, or known by, the Ibiato Sirionó. Although Marta no longer could speak Sirionó and in fact was culturally a Guarayo, her Sirionó parentage qualified her for residence in the village. Edilberto, in need of a spouse, readily accepted her as his mate. René, Marta's son, was already learning Sirionó from his playmates.

While Jack discouraged the Sirionó from living permanently in his old house, preferring instead that they build their own, Edilberto, Marta, and René had settled in for an indefinite stay. They had, in reality, become caseros, or caretakers. Since Edilberto was not known for his prowess as a hunter or his dedication as a farmer, Jack had been paying him a little money to do minor repairs around the house, mixing adobe to fill cracks and holes, replacing roof tiles, and helping keep the weeds down. As long as Edilberto was engaged in these chores, he felt he had a right to remain in the house. His only other option was to build a house of his own now that he had a wife and child (he had been previously living with relatives), a task that required a great deal of effort.

Every day, Edilberto would fix one roof tile or plaster one hole. This usually took the better part of the day with work being sandwiched in between meals, naps, and visiting. When Edilberto was working, every detail required lengthy thought and planning. The execution then took on the surreal characteristics of someone moving under water: he had developed an amazing economy of motion. Sometimes, I would sit nearby while Edilberto was working, but he never had much to say. I suspect he thought of me as a usurper, someone who might threaten his right to remain in the house. It also became apparent that my attempts to make conversation were interpreted as overseeing his work, perhaps to report back on its progress. For several weeks, at the end of the day Edilberto would seek me out to come appraise his labor. When I failed to be critical or make other suggestions, simply telling him that it looked "fine," he finally realized that I wasn't a spy. The repairs became more sporadic as time went on. But Edilberto continued to take a personal interest in the house, and I knew I could depend on him to keep out the cows and pigs and the bands of marauding children who were bent on leveling everything in sight.

Although my relationship with Edilberto eased a bit as he came to understand that I was not in competition with him for the house, he remained distant and formal when we talked. He was basically shy, considered by his peers to be not too bright, and prone to grinning rather than talking. During those first few weeks, we coexisted quietly under the same roof, each coming and going as necessary but not pushing the relationship much farther. Then the army ants invaded.

I was beginning to feel that I had reached some sort of equilibrium with my living conditions. Although the bats still bothered me with their flitting and their constant, high-pitched chatter and bickering, my fear of them was beginning to abate. I had also, with Edilberto's help, blocked up most of the toad holes so they were no longer a nuisance. Then, in the middle of one night, when the power to cope is lowest, army ants invaded my room.

The bats warned me of the invasion with an incredible display of shrieking and flapping. I was asleep when the noise began and, at first, ignored it, but a sense of something amiss began to work its way into my consciousness. What was wrong with those bats? They fought, but nothing like this. Finally, I shot a flashlight beam across the room. The far wall was a seething mass of ants, huge columns of them moving up into the roof, the source of the bats' cries. As I moved the light around, the ants seemed to be everywhere: columns branched out in all directions while thousands of unattached ants hunted randomly. On the floor I could see roaches and spiders writhing in agony as the ants covered and ate them. The table beside my bed that held my clothes was black with ants; they seemed to be sucking on the fabric trying to extract my scent to determine if there was indeed flesh underneath. I sat for a moment fascinated by the spectacle, but my reverie was broken when I realized a column had started up my bedpost and was moving across the top of my mosquito net. A few of the smaller ants had worked their way through the mesh and immediately set about finding any exposed area of skin. Their bite was painful but didn't carry the sting of fire ants. I discovered that by banging my mattress on the bed frame the vibra-

Figure 5

THE ANDERSON HOUSE

FRONT ELEVATION

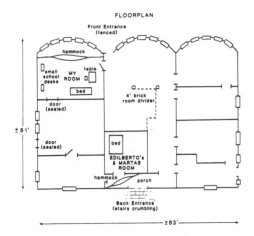

FLOORPLAN

Front Entrance
(fenced)

hammock

small
school   MY   table
desks   ROOM

bed

4' brick
room divider

door
(sealed)

± 51'

door
(sealed)   bed

EDILBERTO's
& MARTAS
ROOM

hammock   porch

Back Entrance
(stairs crumbling)

±63'

→ N

REAR ELEVATION

81

tions that were produced discouraged their forward movement. When enough had retreated that I could safely leave the net, I reached down and shook off my sandals. After I had put them on, I continued to sit cross-legged on the bed, trying to estimate how many steps it would take to reach the door. When I had gathered my wits about me, I sprung off the bed, landed on one foot, took another giant leap and then one more, flinging open the door and rushing into the next room. No ants. I exhaled. Brushing off the ants that I had collected while making my escape, I made my way to Edilberto's room for help.

As I turned a corner from the hallway, I saw that a small kerosene lamp in Marta's and Edilberto's room was burning. Many of the Sirionó, I knew, kept a light burning all night if they had the lamp oil. They didn't like sleeping in the dark. The room contained only one piece of furniture, a bed covered by an old, gray, patched muslin mosquito net. I spoke in the direction of the bed: "Edilberto!" Nothing. "Edilberto!" The rooster and two hens sitting in the corner of the room clucked at me. "Edilberto!" Marta's head appeared from under the net. She was one of the curly-haired Sirionó and her hair stuck out at crazy angles. She blinked once and stared at me. Then René peeked out. Still no Edilberto.

"Where's Edilberto?" I asked. Marta and the boy disappeared under the net. I heard grunts and groans. Finally, Edilberto stuck his head out but his eyes were still closed.

"Come quickly," I hissed in a stage whisper, "The *cazadoras* are here!" He still hadn't opened his eyes. I could hear Marta snoring. "Edilberto!" One eye opened. At least I was making progress. "Get up!" At last, he got up from the bed, found an old flashlight and together we walked down the hallway toward my room.

"Are you sure they're cazadoras? I mean, they could be just ants, you know," said Edilberto. "Believe me, these are cazadoras and they're everywhere, *everywhere!*" That brought a skeptical grunt.

When we reached the door of my room, a large column of ants was moving out of the room toward Edilberto's quarters. "Cazadoras!" "Didn't I tell you?" "Let's see." Edilberto walked barefoot into my room only to emerge a second later hopping around and stamping his feet. He let out a string of Spanish profanity followed by what was probably its equivalent in Sirionó.

"There are a *lot* of ants in there!" "Didn't I tell you?" Edilberto sat down on what had at one time been a brick room divider and stared at his feet.

"What do you think we should do?" Unfortunately, this was his question, not mine. "I don't know. This has never happened to me before. What do you think we should do?" "Well," said Edilberto, "we could throw water on them." "Will that work?" "Probably not. Then there's fire. That always works." "Fire?" I was almost afraid to ask. All my worldly possessions were in that room, not to mention my field notes. "We'll get some dry palm fronds and set them on fire and then brush them over the floor and walls." "But where are we going to get dry palm fronds in the middle of the night?" "Off people's roofs."

By now, Marta and René, finally roused by the noise, had joined us. She agreed that fire would be the best method. The four of us went to several houses, pulling off two or three fronds from each roof. At only one house were the residents aware of our presence. We told them what we needed and why. They expressed their sympathy at our plight and then went back to sleep. When we had gathered our supply of palm leaves, we went back to the house and set them ablaze one at a time, sweeping the room before us as we entered. The ants sounded like popcorn as the flames hit them. We moved the flaming branches so quickly that the fire did not damage anything else. As we moved through the room, the ants began to regroup into the familiar columns, disappearing into holes and cracks in the floor. Within a matter of minutes, they were gone. Edilberto gave me his most ingratiating smile and padded off to bed with Marta and René on his heels.

The next day, Edilberto escorted several of the men through the house, telling them about the night's disaster. Chiro and Vicente were among the group, and they seemed to remember that this had happened before in this particular corner of the house. The men agreed that there must be a nest of the ants under the foundation. (I found this curious, since I had heard that army ants did not stay permanently anywhere.) Chiro poked at a few holes and some ants emerged. I had a sinking feeling in my stomach and could tell when I looked at Edilberto that the same thought was running through his mind. It wasn't over yet.

A week later, the ants marched again. Like the first time, it was at night but earlier. For some reason, there seemed to be fewer of them. I decided to stand my ground, sitting in bed with a flashlight and pounding the mattress every time a column started up the post. After two hours of this, the ant mass began to move to the other side of a room, having hunted out the area where I was. I reflected with sarcastic amusement that I was becoming an expert in army ant behavior: once they had hunted an area, it was unlikely they would return for several days or weeks. I amazed myself by going to sleep while the marauders were working on the other half of my room.

The next morning I told Edilberto that the ants had come again but had moved on quickly. He seemed concerned that his room was probably next. Nothing would get rid of them for good, he said but poison. I didn't have any and didn't know where we could find some in the village. Edilberto suggested I talk to Nancy since she had access to the clinic where he remembered there had been some poison for head lice. Nancy and I checked in the room of the old house that had once served as a clinic and found two small cans of delousing powder. It was DDT—a scourge on the environment but absolutely unbeatable when it comes to killing power. Edilberto and I sprinkled the powder around the perimeter of my room, down likely holes, and outside the house into a wall crack where many of the ants had disappeared. We watched the ants come up and taste the stuff and then return to their tunnels. Within three days there wasn't an ant in sight. Whether the DDT was carried down into the nest and killed it or the ants simply decided to move on once the noxious powder had been spread about I never knew; but the remainder of my stay in Ibiato passed without further invasions.

After we had successfuly met the ant crises, Edilberto's taciturn facade began to erode. While he never was really talkative, the formality receded and we became friends. In the late afternoons, we frequently sat on the porch overlooking the small plaza and chatted while the boys played soccer or tried their skill at bull riding. Edilberto told me that before he began living in Anderson's house, he and Marta had accompanied a group of Sirionó to "colonize" a place known as Santa Fe.

Santa Fe is located in a far corner of the land designated as belonging to the Sirionó. When Jack Anderson first settled the mission, he staked out a territory of about 7,000 hectares for Sirionó use. The land he chose included both grassland for cattle and forest for farming. When the Agrarian Reform was implemented in 1953, Anderson began formal solicitation of title for this property as a Comunidad Indigena (Indigenous Community). But by the time of my arrival in 1982, no title had yet been secured. The reasons for this long delay are many; and in some respects are typical of the problems experienced by anyone in Bolivia who does not have the time or resources to pursue the process to its conclusion. In the Santa Cruz region, for example, agricultural colonists are still waiting for titles to land settled as early as 1964.

Jack had paid for a survey and had pushed the proceedings as far as possible with local authorities in Trinidad. When the case had to be sent to La Paz, he turned over the documents to a Protestant church group working in the capital city. As so often happens, the almost continuous turnover in governments caused constant setbacks. Protestant missions are not known for dealing aggressively with any government, fearing that to do so will risk their expulsion. According to Anderson, the papers had been stalled for several years, but he knew of no other agency that would sponsor the project. After discussing the matter with Jack, I suggested he send the documents to Jürgen Riester, an anthropologist working in Santa Cruz who founded Ayuda para el Campesino Indígena del Oriente Boliviano (APCOB), a grassroots indigenous institute for eastern Bolivian Indians. Riester agreed to take on the Sirionó case and his legal staff became actively involved in the titling process.

In the meantime, the Sirionó continue to fight to retain their land. For the most part, the ranchers who surround them and other individuals residing in the area respect the *mojones* (boundary markers) that delimit Sirionó property, actually two large parcels separated by a lake and a small strip of land belonging to the Universidad Técnica del Beni (see Fig. 6). But there are others, many residing in Casarabe, who are determined to take the land away from the Sirionó. Most people in support of this move simply resented the fact that Indians held property. Their attitude was that "Choris" don't need (i.e., deserve) that much land and would probably be better off working on local farms and ranches as peons where they could be "taken care of." In many cases, attempts to gain control of Sirionó property are not motivated by a need for the land but by a desire to take it away from the Indians.

So far, legal maneuvers to take the land from the Sirionó have been thwarted by the intervention of an agrarian judge in Trinidad who is sympathetic to keeping their holdings intact. Since the law recognizes squatters' rights once land has been cleared and a structure built, there have been attempts to invade Sirionó territory and occupy it before anyone is aware that outsiders have moved in. On one occasion, the Sirionó had advance warning; they were there to meet the group when it arrived, and the invaders retreated. The next episode took place in 1981 at Santa Fe, one of the more remote areas of the property. A cattle shed built at night by a small band of men was discovered the next day by Sirionó hunters. They returned that night and burned it down. Word of this quickly spread to Casarabe and the invasion was once again halted. Burning down a building, for whatever reason, is considered a highly aggressive act, and not all Sirionó were in favor of responding in this fashion. Nevertheless, the result was to stay further advances for several years.

The people of Casarabe still tend to think of the Sirionó as bárbaros, savages, and stories of their past raids continue to circulate among residents of the town. Having an entire community of Sirionó located only five kilometers from Casarabe's doorstep is no doubt a frequent source of consternation. The burning of the cattle shed was interpreted as an act of war, obviously blown out of proportion; nonetheless it reinforced ideas held by the residents of Casarabe that the Sirionó are only "partially civilized." Although the Sirionó do not want to be regarded as Choris (backward, uncivilized, and traitorous, as they were so often described by mestizos), they also know that the element of fear has effectively kept many mestizos at bay. Shortly before I arrived, rumor reached Ibiato that another invasion was in the works. With Anderson's urging, several families were sent to colonize, or rather, recolonize Santa Fe. Edilberto, Marta, and René were asked to join the group since they had not yet constructed a house in Ibiato.

Santa Fe is situated on another Moxos mound, similar to Ibiato but

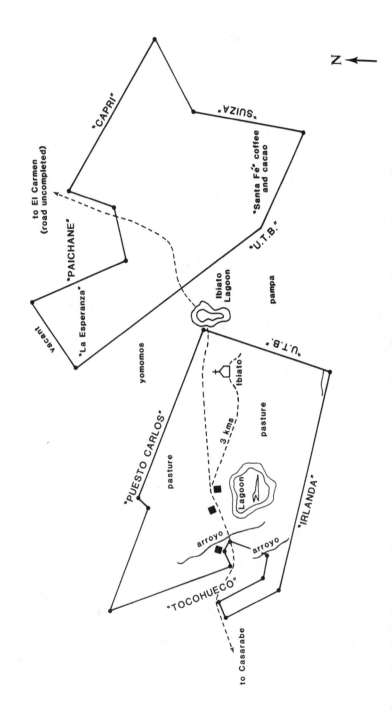

Figure 6

Map of Holding of

THE INDIGENOUS COMMUNITY OF IBIATO
canton SAN JAVIER Prov. CERCADO dept. BENI

scale 1:30,000

smaller in size. It is located about 15 kilometers southwest of the village and is difficult to reach because of a large swamp. In the 1950s, Jack settled twenty or thirty families there to alleviate some tensions in Ibiato and to protect the area from squatters. The land was cleared and planted with cacao and coffee trees. After a few years, the settlement failed. Many of the residents died from disease and the survivors returned to Ibiato. Edilberto told me that coffee and chocolate are still harvested, although it is a long, hard trip to Santa Fe and most people do not want to remain there overnight. When Edilberto and Marta went to Santa Fe to reestablish a settlement there, the group stayed only long enough to clear a little land and build a few shelters, making the place look inhabited. Then they all returned to Ibiato, much to the disgust of Anderson and the village leaders. There were just too many *bultos* (shapeless forms) and *tigres* (jaguars) around, Edilberto said. The bultos are spirits of the Sirionó who died and are buried there, according to Edilberto and others. They come out at night and walk around, frightening everyone. Marta said that no one slept very much. Then, because the place is surrounded by thick coffee bushes and cacao trees, it is an ideal haunt for jaguars. Each morning the men found tracks in the woods near their camp. As soon as some sign of human habitation had been left, Edilberto and his colleagues hurried back to Ibiato. They had no intention of remaining there to establish a permanent outpost even though most agreed the land was good for farming.

Now there were more rumors and the ererecuas convened a meeting. This was the first public meeting called since my arrival. Because only men were present, I was hesitant to intrude. I noticed that Edilberto did not attend. "Why are the men meeting?" I asked. "They want people to go to Santa Fe again. To live there. But no one wants to go."

I left Edilberto and walked over to Nancy's house where we could watch the meeting in progress. Daniel and Arturo, the village leaders, were standing in front of the group, alternately speaking to the men who were standing up against a low wall on one side of the plaza. We could see that there was disagreement. Finally, the meeting broke up and the men returned to their houses. It appeared that for the present at least, the resettlement of Santa Fe would remain unresolved.

Chiro came back to the house smiling and shaking his head. He repeated what Edilberto had said, that no one wanted to live in Santa Fe. Not only were they afraid, he said, but it was too far away from everything. People didn't want to live that way any more. Then I asked him about Daniel and Arturo. Why were there two ererecuas in Ibiato, both with apparently equal power, serving simultaneously? And what was the nature of leadership in the community? Chiro could tell me only part of the story; Jack added another piece, and the remainder was filled in by events that occurred while I was in the village.

"Daniel"

EIGHT
Chapter 8

Whehen Thomas Anderson and his sons Paul and Jack decided to build their mission at the site the Sirionó called the place of high ground, Ibiato, in about 1932, they had four families with them from Buen Jesús, near what would become Casarabe. Shortly after Ibiato was founded, an ererecua nicknamed "Choco" (light-skinned) brought his band of forty to fifty people to Ibiato. They had been enslaved on the Arias ranch in Santa Cruz but had escaped and made their way north to the Beni. They vastly outnumbered the other inhabitants at Ibiato, so Choco became the new ererecua. He stayed in power just a few years, until he died of pneumonia. In the meantime, another erarecua and his group were brought by Jack to Ibiato. This was Eo (hand) who had a full beared, was dark-skinned, intelligent, and kind. He had five wives and was considered to be at least as powerful as Choco. While Choco was alive, he had to share some of his power with Eo. And so began the tradition of having two ererecuas serving simultaneously in Ibiato.

Anderson recited this history when I asked him why Ibiato had two leaders. The Sirionó in Ibiato either did not remember or, more likely, did not associate the historical precedent with the current leadership structure. They answered the question in another way, but one that from their perspective is equally correct. Since the Sirionó are now sedentary horticulturists, the ererecua cannot be continually present among them as was true in the past. Nowadays, an ererecua must spend weeks at a time out in the chacos, clearing his fields for planting and caring for his crops until harvest. Then there may be periods of two or three days when he goes on a hunt or must leave the village for other reasons. During these times it is expected that the other ererecua will remain in Ibiato to take care of any problems that might arise. Still, I found it a curious custom that grew out of the mission environment where several bands that normally would have remained autonomous were forced to live together. During Ibiato's early years, each ererecua would enter into competition with the others to achieve control over the entire population. While a "first" and "second" ererecua would be acknowledged, each band's leader retained a following among his own local group. Loyalties to individual bands, however, became more diffuse over time. Public recognition of the pecking order of ererecuas occurred during the circle dance and accompanying chants. Each leader would give over to one of higher status, with the most powerful ererecua finishing the chant.

In the tradition of band political organization, leadership is by consensus. Men lead only as long as people are willing to follow. To a large extent, the Sirionó ererecuas are also consensual leaders, depending on personal attributes and charisma to maintain their positions of authority. Nonetheless, as Chiro explained, these qualities alone were not enough. A man had to come from a "chiefly" family to be considered a potential leader. These were men who could trace a direct relationship to a former ererecua, preferably through an unbroken male line. Ideally, an ererecua was the son of an ererecua. If his father had been powerful, then the son had a better chance of being selected, assuming he also had the necessary personal attributes for leadership. I asked Chiro if a case had ever occurred where someone who was personally popular but not of the "chiefly line" had attempted to become an ererecua. He answered that several of the younger men, particularly those who had spent time away from Ibiato and chafed under the old traditions, had attempted to gain office but had failed. In the end, even those who originally had supported the young contenders agreed that they could not be taken seriously—no one would ever obey them. Age was also a factor in selecting a leader, since the ererecua was "paba," father, of the band. While age was not venerated, it was respected; and most people I talked to agreed that part of being a successful ererecua was being able to project an image of wisdom and experience—qualities, they felt, that normally came with age.

I also discovered that many of these leadership characteristics were defined in terms of the individuals presently in office. If sweetness and kindness were attributes of one ererecua, then these were admirable qualities. If toughness and meanness described the other, then these too were acceptable—assuming, of course, that each leader was in favor at the time. If not, these same qualities could be used as points of criticism. The position of ererecua, once achieved, had no guarantees of longevity. It was apparent from conversations I had with many of the villagers that their leaders would remain in office only as long as their constituents suffered their presence. One or two, I was told, simply quit out of frustration with the job. Because of the nature of the system, the ererecuas were always subject to pressure by factions in the village, to attempts to manipulate them, and, inevitably, the playing off of one ererecua against the other. It seemed a very divisive system but one that nevertheless was consistent with Sirionó personality and attitudes. Having two leaders meant that neither could claim absolute authority, resulting in a system of checks and balances of sorts. Then, too, if one ererecua refused to support a certain point of view, there was possible recourse with the other. Leadership was therefore very fluid, just as it had been during precontact times. While people might have been critical of a particular ererecua in office, no one challenged the system itself. No matter the origin of the tradition of having two leaders, it has become accepted and institutionalized in Ibiato.

Although I did not witness the ouster of one leader and the installation of another, such a case occurred shortly before my arrival. Eloy Erachendu, one of the ererecuas, went through a long period of drinking bouts, angering people and failing to meet his responsibilities and obligations as a leader. In spite of the years of prohibition against alcohol, drinking in the village became commonplace once Anderson left. Because of Ibiato's Protestant origins and continuing identification with fundamentalist Christianity, alcohol use has never been condoned or accepted as proper behavior, even by those who drink. Drinking by an ererecua is criticized, but for the most part, tolerated unless the man becomes abusive or the drinking becomes excessive. In Eloy's case, his frequent drunkenness became a source of disgruntlement among the villagers. As continues to be the practice in times of extreme crisis, word was sent to Jack that he was needed in Ibiato. Upon his arrival, the community was convened to discuss the problem. As far as I could determine, Anderson's role in this meeting was basically that of mediator. Names were presented, discussed, or challenged. At the end of the evening a consensus was reached: Arturo Eanta, son of the deceased ererecua Eanta (hard, mean) would be the new leader. His nomination had been accompanied by considerable dissent because he, too, was a known drinker. The names of some of the younger men had been proposed but for the most part had been dismissed for lack of maturity or confidence in their abilities. The impression left was that Arturo won by default. He would take his place, nonetheless, beside Daniel Mayachare, a weak but kind ererecua who was generally viewed as a peacemaker.

The most frequent responsibility of the ererecua is the settlement of disputes; if both are present, it is done in tandem. If a particularly troublesome case is presented and an ererecua is absent, the other may put off attempting to resolve the issue until the absent leader returns. Very few incidents are brought into the public domain. While nothing can be kept secret in Ibiato, most problems are dealt with in the privacy of the houses of those involved. Once apprised of a dispute, the ererecuas will walk together to the litigants' houses to try to obtain an acceptable, equitable resolution.

Because ererecuas have no real coercive power unless backed by the entire village, their role is that of mediator and counselor, not enforcer. Much of their time is spent in arbitrating domestic disputes during which the counseling role becomes paramount. In these cases, the two religious leaders, Chiro and Vicente, may also be consulted, making the domestic disturbance a moral issue as well. Because Ibiato continues to be a religiously based community, an attempt will always be made to deal with a particular situation in the context of Christian philosophy and teachings, albeit with a Sirionó interpretation.

From the perspective of state or provincial government, the ererecuas at Ibiato are officially recognized civil authorities. Therefore, it is they who must interact with the outside world as representatives of their village in the national political system. Ibiato is fortunate in one respect: as an indigenous community it is not involved with political parties. In mestizo communities, the mayor *(alcalde)*, police chief *(intendente)*, and possibly other officials will change with each new government in power. It is also not uncommon for these offices to be filled by outsiders as part of the political patronage system. So far, Ibiato has maintained its autonomy in selecting leaders, without outside interference.

The remaining duties of the ererecuas relate to the organization of labor for community work projects. It is in this area that their authority may be put to the greatest test. Again, as consensual leaders, they can request that people work but can do little if they refuse, as happened in the attempted resettlement of Santa Fe. Communal labor was not an element of aboriginal culture, having been imposed as part of the mission routine. Nowadays, the church bell may be rung once or twice a month calling the men to work so that weeds can be cut down, a fence line replaced, the school or church roof repaired, or the old bridge crossing the arroyo at the base of the mound refitted. Depending on the nature of the task or the time of the year, the turnout can range from 40 to 80 percent of the male population. If several work days go by with unusually poor attendance, the ererecuas may call on the two pastors, Chiro and Vicente, to admonish and encourage their parishioners to become more involved in community affairs.

The fact that the pastors may be asked to intercede in secular matters is an indication that a parallel system of authority exists. In recent years, religious leadership has been viewed more and more as equal in importance to that of the ererecuas. It is also possible that the position of pastor may become a stepping-stone for civil leadership. Both Chiro and Vicente are sons of deceased ererecuas, so are eligible for the office. With their experience as religious leaders they have gained public visibility, making them strong contenders as future ererecuas. To date, the role of pastor has been treated as complementary to that of ererecua, not competitive. For the time being, at least, the two systems coexist peacefully.

Religious leadership among the Sirionó is a relatively recent phenomenon. When Anderson lived in Ibiato, he was the acknowledged head of the village and religious leader. The ererecuas answered ultimately to him and he had a great deal to say in their selection. The need to have Jack's presence even today is an affirmation of his continued influence in legitimizing the process. The practice of training Sirionó as religious leaders came with Perry Priest, a missionary with the Summer Institute of Linguistics (SIL). Perry and his wife Anne had lived periodically in San Pedro de Richards, returning to their headquarters in Riberalta, Tumi Chuqua, with several Sirionó families to assist with Bible translation. While producing a Bible in Sirionó was the manifest reason for bringing the Sirionó to Riberalta, they would also receive formal training in Christian dogma and leadership.

When conditions at San Pedro began to deteriorate with the change in ranch management, Perry arranged for several of the families to move to Ibiato. Because the Andersons had long since gone to Trinidad, the Priests felt free to relocate their translation work in Ibiato where they were assured a stable supply of informants. It is also likely that the Priests viewed Ibiato as a last refuge for the Sirionó; and since so much time and effort had been invested to that point in linguistic studies, it was reasonable that they would want to focus on this remaining settlement for their missionary work. Once in Ibiato, Perry selected several of the younger men to assist him with Bible translation and also to train as future teachers and religious leaders. These men, along with their families, were taken to Tumi Chuqua for several months at a time. To be selected to go to Riberalta became a sought-after goal among the Sirionó, rather like a trip to summer camp. Since wives and children could be brought along, there was no wrenching loneliness. Participants received expense money, were given clothing, had comfortable but familiar housing, and ate well. There were almost continuous activities scheduled between classwork and linguistic sessions: volleyball, soccer, singing, and, of course, prayer meetings. While at Tumi Chuqua, the Sirionó also met representatives from other lowland Bolivian native peoples who were there for the same purpose. For most, this experience was their first in thinking in a positive way about their Indian heritage.

One of the early participants in the Tumi Chuqua project was Chiro Cuellar. Perry had quickly singled him out as a potential leader because of his easy manner in dealing with his peers and his quick intelligence. Chiro became Priest's primary informant and was rewarded with trips to various conferences, including one in Panama. Later, when I met Perry in Ibiato, he said he now believed it was wrong to remove native people from their own environment. "It ruins them," he said. "They become misfits in their own culture." But, he admitted, Chiro was an exception. He had taken all the travel and attention in stride, storing it away for perhaps some future reference but sliding easily back into life in Ibiato. This outlook, according to Perry, was not due to anything he might have done but was rather a reflection of Chiro's unique character.

Of all Ibiato's leaders, past or present, secular or religious, Chiro has the potential of becoming the most influential man in his community. Like most Sirionó at Ibiato below the age of forty, Chiro is literate and bilingual. But because of his special relationship with Priest, he has gained a broader perspective of the world and consequently possesses a great deal of self-confidence in dealing with non-Sirionó. Outside Ibiato, many of the other men, including the ererecuas, succumb to old patterns of humility and deference toward mestizos, hanging back, mumbling, staring at their feet, and always speaking carefully. While not appearing aggressive or cocky, Chiro does none of these things. He treats mestizos as equals, not superiors, looking them straight in the eye. His height (over six feet) makes him an imposing sight, particularly when mounted on his big bay stallion. But it is the frequent smile and easy manner that ultimately win people over. All this, of course, is simply a measure of the level of his acculturation. He has learned to function in the larger Bolivian society to a degree that many of his peers have not attained.

Perhaps because his is a wider universe, Chiro consciously reflects on the precarious situation of Ibiato. He fears that when Jack Anderson dies, Ibiato may not be able to hold itself together. Perry Priest left Bolivia in 1984, with the phasing out of SIL in that country. Anderson and Priest were the village's most effective advocates in dealing with Bolivian society, Jack in the realm of regional politics and Perry at the national level. With or without his knowledge or consent, Chiro has been groomed to take over at least some of this advocacy. In talking with Chiro about his becoming an ererecua, it was clear that he is uncomfortable with the responsibilities the office may bring. Because of his charisma, his ability to deal with mestizos, and his position as pastor, Chiro, in spite of his age, has already been asked to consider becoming an ererecua. He has refused. When the time comes that he must accept the nomination, he will not disappoint his people, but he is aware that Ibiato's very survival may rest ultimately on his shoulders alone. He knows that his particular skills, matched by no one, could eclipse those of any other ererecua in power, and that by emerging as the single most powerful ererecua of the village he could also radically alter Ibiato's long-standing system of dual leadership. Chiro contemplates this possiblity with both anticipation and dread. For now, he is prudent in not letting his personal power undermine the authority of the ererecuas. There seems to be an innate understanding that part of keeping Ibiato intact and therefore able to fend off continuing pressure from the outside lies in preserving those traditions that act as a binding force in community life.

In his role as pastor, Chiro remains low-keyed. It took me several Sundays in church to understand how his power as a religious leader is orchestrated. The service invariably consists of opening hymns, announcements, individual or group presentations in front of the congregation, the Bible reading and sermon, and closing hymns. Vicente, not Chiro, opened and closed the service, made the announcements, and generally regulated the pace. At first, I perceived Vicente's role as being the more important, primarily because he stood in front of the church and was heard from most often. As time passed, it became evident that Vicente was more like a master of ceremonies whose primary task was to introduce the main event, Chiro. The most meaningful and significant part of the service is the reading, explanation, and commentary of the day's Bible passage. Because of his extensive training, Chiro is considered the most qualified to do this. He was well instructed by SIL to interpret passages from the Bible in terms that the Sirionó can understand and relate to. Chiro also has a certain presence when speaking to the congregation that others recognize. Without appearing pretentious, he projects a depth of understanding and confidence that can come only from intensive study. When the Bible portion is over, Chiro returns to his seat at the back of the church, but it is clear that his was the most important part of the service.

Because he is gregarious by nature, Chiro takes his pastoring seriously, spending each morning and afternoon visiting one or two families. These are not pastoral visits in a rigid sense, where moral issues or religious topics are discussed. They are visits that primarily affirm friendship, trust, and unity—and that everyone matters. These visits are often accompanied by storytelling and peals of raucous laughter, which greatly enhance Chiro's standing as a leader among equals. There are family rivalries and divisions between drinkers and nondrinkers, but Chiro somehow manages to cut across these lines by offering friendship to everyone.

In addition to his pastoral duties, Chiro is expected more and more to play the role of cultural broker. Because the ererecuas are the official agents of the community in dealing with the outside world, Chiro must be careful not to appear to be superseding their authority in this realm. On a community level, most interactions are with Casarabe, the only settlement within easy walking or riding distance from Ibiato. Since Casarabe is located on a major market route, it is the service center for the region surrounding it. Staples such as sugar, salt, lard, flour, and kerosene can be obtained in Casarabe, and there are places to buy cold beer, sodas and gelatin dessert, and, of course, drinking establishments to purchase and consume cane alcohol. The Sirionó frequent Casarabe to buy supplies and to "go to town." Repeated efforts to form a community store in Ibiato have failed. The relationship between the two towns, however, is guarded. The mestizos of Casarabe consider the Sirionó to be inferior; they are "Chori," and they have the audacity to hold their own land. The Sirionó distrust the Casarabe residents because they are mestizos, and mestizos always denigrate and take advantage of Indians.

Through their various interactions with the Sirionó, it has become known among the Casarabeños that issues concerning Ibiato are best dealt with through Chiro. They express this in such terms as "He is more like us, you know, *entendido* [logical, intelligent]." It is also common for Chiro to accompany Daniel and Arturo to Casarabe or even Trinidad in activities concerning official documents. Neither ererecua is literate, and their expertise with government matters is limited. Thus there is an expectation among local mestizos and Sirionó as well that Chiro will be the go-between, the bridge between their two cultures.

During my four months in Ibiato, three mestizos visited the village. On each occasion, Chiro was their initial contact (as he was mine). The first visitor was Don "Vilo" (Wilfredo) Saucedo, one of the "elite" of Casarabe. He is a member of a well-known Santa Cruz-Beni family and owns the largest store and bar-restaurant in town. Vilo asked Chiro if Ibiato had a *corregidor* (magistrate). Chiro responded in the negative; there were only the two caciques (this term is used with outsiders who are not familiar with the Sirionó word ererecua). I noted with interest that Chiro named Arturo Eanta first, the more aggressive of the two. Chiro offered Vilo a chair in the shade and the two sat down to discuss the problem. Pedro "Chuchú" Pepe, Chiro's closest neighbor, had sold the same cow twice during an extended drinking bout in Casarabe. Although none of the Sirionó have large cattle holdings, some of the men have acquired a few head which are run on the savanna between Ibiato and Casarabe. Others may acquire a cow or two from time to time, usually in payment for labor. The bar owners, including Vilo, know when the Sirionó have cattle and will ply them with drink until they are unable to think clearly. At that point, the Sirionó is encouraged to trade his cow to pay for the alcohol already consumed and to buy more. This time, however, Chuchú sold the same cow twice, once to Vilo and later to another man to cover his drinking debts. The second buyer actually got the cow, infuriating Vilo once he realized he had been duped. Chuchú was so drunk he probably was unaware of having sold his cow to two different people. Vilo Saucedo was in Ibiato to bring Chuchú to justice.

After Chiro understood the details of the case, he took Vilo to Arturo's house. Since Chuchú was away from Ibiato, the problem had to be resolved in his absence. Later, Chiro told me that Chuchú would not be arrested. He,

Vicente (who now takes care of the town's cattle herd), Arturo, and Daniel offered Vilo the pick of the herd in exchange for dropping the matter. Vilo got his cow and Chuchú was off the hook. He would be asked to work some land for the community to pay back the value of the cow, but Chiro said Chuchú probably would forget about it by then. Chiro obviously disliked the entire affair as did the ererecuas; but if they can intercede in any way, no Sirionó is ever turned over to mestizo justice.

The remaining two visitors were local ranchers who stopped by Ibiato to look for ranch hands. Again, each man went directly to Chiro who, after offering them his hospitality, directed them to the two ererecuas. All three of these visitors were noticeably uncomfortable with being in a village of "Choris." They stayed close to Chiro as someone they felt they could relate to. Chiro was also one of the few people in the village who could offer visiting mestizos some of the comforts they were accustomed to receiving; a real chair, not a log stool or a string hammock; a table, china dishes, and forks, not a big spoon and a chipped, enameled tin plate.

While Chiro is well liked and respected, his greater economic success and material possessions are also a source of envy among the villagers. Ibiato, like most peasant communities, ascribes to what George Foster calls the "Image of Limited Good," the idea that worthwhile things come in limited amounts—if someone has more, then it must be at his neighbor's expense. Chiro is a successful cultural broker and advocate for Ibiato because in many ways he has bought into the white man's system, which includes a desire to accumulate wealth. In keeping with their aboriginal traditions, most Sirionó do not delay gratification. Consequently, if they acquire cattle, the animals are usually slaughtered and eaten soon after or sold for cash which can be spent. The same is generally true of wages earned or money that comes from crops or game animal skins—it is spent almost as soon as it is in hand. Chiro, however, saves his money and manages his resources carefully, contrary to the patterns of his neighbors. He invests in cattle, horses, and riding oxen which are accumulated over time.

For a while, Chiro managed the communal herd, eventually becoming disgusted with the town's attitudes and turning the chore over to Vicente. This herd, started by Anderson to help with mission expenses and to provide beef on special occasions, at one time numbered over 150 head but has been rapidly depleted over the years from too frequent consumption and cases like Chuchú's. The villagers, however, could only see Chiro's herd increasing while the communal herd diminished in size. It was obvious from their perspective that Chiro's success must be at their expense. When the gossip reached disturbing proportions, Chiro in exasperation handed the job of managing the herd to Vicente. The result has been an even faster decrease in animals from lack of proper attention and Vicente's tendency to give in to requests to slaughter more frequently.

The communal herd has been a long-standing source of friction in Ibiato, stemming again from Sirionó desire for immediate gratification. The fact that the herd acts as a reserve bank account and safety net for the village is largely unrecognized by the inhabitants. For them, it is simply unexploited meat. Arturo, Daniel, Chiro, and Vicente are constantly under pressure to divide up what cattle are left and distribute them among the residents. Because there has never been a real shortage of meat, the village leaders, with Jack's support, so far have resisted. Hunting continues to provide almost all of the community's animal protein intake, a tradition not likely to be replaced by animal husbandry. The Sirionó have always been hunters and hunting continues to give pleasure, satisfaction, and status in a way that farming or ranching never will.

"Chiro"

A Siriono' hunter and his son in the vicinity of Ibiato in 1941.
(Photo by Raymond Crist)

Siriono´ men performing the Hito-Hito dance and chant. Ibiato, 1941. (Photo by Raymond Crist)

The Guarayo woman, Concha, who kept me company in Salvatierra and who knew of the whereabouts of Holmberg's guide, Luís Silva Sánchez.

The canoe that took me up the Río Blanco in search of Holmberg's guide.

View from the Río Blanco of a small riverbank homestead, or *barraca*.

One of the community-held cows is slaughtered after villagers pressure the *ererecuas* to dispose of it. The *ererecua* Daniel can be seen at the rear, right, overseeing the animal's disposition.

Nancy, her children, and neighbors assist in the soaking and peeling of coffee beans, picked from trees in Ibatio. Some of the beans will be sold, but the remainder will be roasted for local consumption.

A Siriono couple winnows rice they are hulling in a *tacu*, a large wood mortar. This process is usually carried out in the open, where the wind can blow away the chaff.

A typical Siriono dwelling in Ibatio. Houses are small and minimally enclosed, but they do provide a sleeping place and shelter from the elements. The two women are carrying water from a nearby creek.

Nancy, Chiro, and Nancy's brother, Wilson, navigate through the soggy Beni pampa. Chiro is using his riding ox.

Chiro and son Pepe display deer hides that have been staked to dry in the sun. These will be sold to Don Alberto, the itinerant trader.

The Trinidad-Casarabe road after only a few days rain.

A Sirionó woman stands in the door of her wattle-and-daub house. A *tacu* has been placed across the doorway to keep out pigs that roam the village.

Nancy and a neighbor prepare *biscochos* made from hand-ground cornmeal. The box frame in the foreground is a flour sifter made from old window screens.

Three Siriono' brothers gather in the shade of their house to play games after school.

Perhaps the oldest living Siriono, Ignacia Cuasu, retells the story of her capture by the Yanaiguas.

Nancy's step-father, Demetrio, prepares a new *mano* (pestle) for the family *tacu*.

A group of Sirionó pose for a photo on a Sunday afternoon. At the far left is the schoolteacher, Nataniel, with his radio. Arturo, one of the *ererecuas*, stands next to the young teacher.

The long trail to the outlying *chacos* (fields) where the Sirionó grow their crops.

Two Siriono´ children tend a pot stewing meat. Even today, children learn to be self-sufficient at an early age.

NINE
Chapter 9

In 1940 when Allan Holmberg studied the Sirionó, they were, above all else, hunters. At that time they did practice some horticulture, but the Sirionó were never enthusiastic farmers. Their techniques were crude, consisting of little more than finding a place in the forest where a large tree had fallen, leaving clear a small space of ground that could be planted to corn, manioc, or sweet potatoes. A few months later, the Sirionó would return to harvest what was left after insects, rodents, and weeds had taken their toll.

Vegetable foods, both cultivated and wild, were important to the Sirionó diet, but the desired food was meat, and to obtain it in sufficient amounts required almost constant movement. Sirionó men hunted with a longbow made of *chonta* palm wood and arrows of reed, bamboo, and chonta. The bows reached two meters or more in length with arrows of equal size, a characteristic peculiar to the Sirionó. Although killing game was a man's task, the women frequently accompanied the men to help call monkeys, spot animals and track them, and carry meat back to camp. After a few days or a week at most, the game would thin out in the area being hunted and the group would move on. A man's worth was measured by his ability to hunt. If he were of a chiefly line, his skill as a hunter would guarantee that he, too, would become *paba*, an ererecua. In time, his expertise as a hunter might also gain him additional wives, a badge of high status. Now, the Sirionó have given up their nomadic existence, but the importance of hunting dominates their lives. Men no longer have multiple spouses and bow hunting has largely been abandoned, replaced by shotguns and rifles. But just as in the past, the young men who are good hunters earn respect from their peers; and although hunting ability alone does not confer leadership, it is a positive factor in selecting any man otherwise qualified.

Hunting in modern-day Bolivia has taken new directions for the Sirionó. In addition to supplying meat, many game animals have skins that can be sold for money or supplies. While I was in Ibiato, in the period between crops, the sale of skins provided the primary source of cash income to villagers other than wage labor. Unfortunately, the Sirionó do not reap the profits they could from their hunting efforts. Many of the animals they hunt are on endangered species lists, and, unlike other nations that give indigenous peoples the right to selectively hunt many of these animals, Bolivia makes no such distinction. Consequently, in order to sell their hides, the Sirionó must work through a contraband network of dealers who pay the necessary "fees" to government officials. Next to wildcat skins, the jaguar being the most prized, *caimanes*, or South American alligators, bring in the highest returns. It is the *contrabandistas*, not the hunters, who make the greatest profit from the sale of animal skins.

One afternoon, Nancy asked me if I would like to go caiman hunting with Chiro and her. I had been on other types of hunts, but had never seen how alligators were taken. At dusk, Chiro saddled up his two riding oxen. He rode the smaller one and Nancy and I the larger. Chiro had his .22 rifle, a machete, and a flashlight. We rode down the trail from town toward the road, cutting off into a large mango grove before reaching the junction. By now the last daylight was gone, and once we were under the cover of the trees it was pitch black. Even the normally placid oxen were anxious at the darkness around them.

When we reached the far edge of the mango grove, Chiro stopped, dismounted, and told us to do the same. We tied the oxen and started out on foot. Soon we were in the midst of a swamp. The trail was now under water and the growth very dense. It was like walking through a tunnel as we moved along single file. At one point Chiro stopped and cut a long pole. I wasn't certain what it was for. Then he told Nancy and me to wait while he went deeper into the swamp. In a few minutes he returned, pulling a canoe behind him. The pole was to propel us through the shallow water. Once in the canoe I felt more at ease. I poured the water out of my boots and soon my feet were warm again. Gliding through the swamp in a canoe was much less threatening than slogging through it on foot, so I sat back to enjoy the sounds and smells of the night. Suddenly we broke out of the swamp into a spectacular universe of stars. For an instant I wondered if we had crossed some threshold of reality; it was as if we were floating through the sky. Then I realized we were on a *yomomal*, a lake covered with floating grass, and that the grass was infested with hundreds of thousands of lightning bugs. In the black of the night, they looked just like the stars above them. Even Nancy and Chiro who had seen the sight many times before hesitated a moment to take in the scene around them.

We poled slowly and quietly through the grass, Chiro sweeping the light back and forth over the lake. He was looking for the telltale reflection of eyes peering above the water. We came upon two or three small caimanes but Chiro passed them by. He told me to listen for their barking, imitating the sound to call them nearer to us. Finally, after two hours of poling, we pulled up beside an animal of acceptable size. It wasn't much of a hunt: Chiro simply held the animal with his light, put the rifle to its head, and pulled the trigger. The caiman rolled over on his back and Chiro grabbed it by the tail, throwing it into the bottom of the canoe. I was disappointed: it couldn't have been more than a meter long. Chiro told me that most of the full-grown animals had been hunted out on this lake because it was so close to the village. The caimanes did travel from one water source to another, however, so there was always hope of bagging a large one even here.

We got only one more caiman that night, only slightly larger than the first. I was bothered that such immature animals were being taken, but I also realized that conservation is a luxury the Sirionó can't afford. As part of Bolivia's consumer economy, they need cash to buy clothing, kerosene, flour, sugar, medicines, and guns and shells to continue hunting. Under these circumstances, anything is fair game.

It was nearly 2 a.m. when we returned to the oxen for the ride back to Ibiato. When we arrived in the village, Chiro tied the two caimanes up in a tree so the dogs wouldn't rip into them. Early the next morning he took off the soft side strips of the hide, the only part which is of value since the back and belly are too horny for use. The four strips of hide were salted and rolled up—the only skins treated in this way. All others, from fur-bearing animals, are stretched and pegged to the ground or put on racks to dry in the sun.

A few days later, Don Adolfo arrived from Casarabe. Adolfo Mercado is a florid, heavy-set man who makes his living as a trader among the small settlements around Casarabe. Although Don Adolfo "buys low and sells high," as is customary among itinerant merchants, he is considered honest and trustworthy. He has been coming to Ibiato for almost ten years and depends on his reputation among the villagers for much of his business. Adolfo also engages in a certain amount of credit trading, particularly for the promise of hides. Dealers such as Adolfo speculate in this market and can make huge profits simply by waiting for prices to go up for specific animals. The most common item bought on credit is alcohol, and many Sirionó will gladly go into debt for a few days drinking and merrymaking.

When Adolfo rode into Ibiato once or twice a week, he had two pack horses loaded with supplies. Chiro brought out his alligator skins, a collared peccary hide, and one large deerskin. Adolfo examined them carefully for damage and measured their length and width. There was no haggling over the price. Adolfo offered US $12 for all and Chiro accepted. Some he spent on supplies that Don Adolfo had spread over a rubber poncho on the ground. Chiro purchased six .22 shells, a liter of kerosene, a kilo of sugar, and some salt. The remainder of his money he put away in his house. Other men followed this same pattern, exchanging hides for cash and merchandise. By midmorning, Adolfo had exhausted his supply of customers, so he loaded up his horses and departed for Casarabe. He carried with him three deerskins, six peccary, and one ocelot hide in addition to the caiman skins sold to him by Chiro.

When they were available, Don Adolfo also bought other products from the Sirionó: wild honey collected in the forest and placed in old bottles with corncob stoppers; roasted palm fruits or other fruits in season; coffee and cacao beans; ostrich (rhea) feathers; and some specialty items requested by residents of Casarabe or Trinidad that could only be procured in the forest by those who knew where to look—herbal remedies, turtle oil, the fat from stingrays, and other products of the wilderness. Folk remedies are still in great demand by the peasantry and by many urban people as well, and they will pay good prices for those items. Don Adolfo acts as a middleman in the marketing of forest products, making a small profit but more than anything enjoying the goodwill of his clientele.

Although animal hides provide an important source of income to the Sirionó, their primary purpose in hunting continues to be to obtain meat. Like other peasant farmers in the lowlands, the Sirionó keep pigs, chickens, and a few ducks. Some, like Chiro, also have a few head of cattle. Nevertheless, these animals do not provide a constant source of animal protein. Most Bolivian peasant families I have known do not eat much meat; it is expensive to buy if it is available at all. Since farm animals compete for resources such as grains, relatively few are kept. Meat thus becomes a "feast" food, and animals are slaughtered infrequently. The typical lowland Bolivian peasant diet consists mainly of rice, corn, plantains, and manioc. The Sirionó, on the other hand, continue to have diets rich in meat. Most families I surveyed had meat in their houses an average of four days a week. Part of the explanation for this is that the Sirionó will search for and consume animals which most lowlanders consider starvation food only: tortoises, monkeys, and small, bony fish. The other reasons behind their high animal protein intake are to be found in the particular social and environmental situation in which they live.

From the earliest European settlement, the Beni has been a cattle region. With grasslands comprising as much as 80 percent of the department's territory, ranching became the leading source of income for the non-native population. Farming has always been of secondary importance primarily because savannas are difficult if not impossible to cultivate using traditional slash-and-burn techniques. Nonetheless, some crops, primarily for subsistence, are grown in the bands of forest along waterways and on "*islas,*" the patches of wooded areas interspersed among the pampas. Typically, it is the mestizo population which has controlled the cattle industry while the indigenous peasantry produced the foodstuffs necessary to feed themselves and ranch personnel.

The area of the Beni that the Sirionó inhabit, the east-central region, is about evenly distributed between forest and pasture. It is also more sparsely populated, particularly by indigenous groups, then the area west of Trinidad. These patterns are noteworthy because it is the native peasantry that is most dependent on game animals as a source of meat and income. In the western region, according to anthropologist James Jones, the competition for those animals has led to the virtual extermination of many species.

For the Sirionó, hunting continues to be good. They are not competing with significant numbers of other people for game resources in the region. Sirionó land is surrounded by large ranches whose owners supply adequate beef to workers as part of their monthly *ración* (kerosene, salt, sugar, flour, etc.). These workers are also earning salaries along with their monthly rations so have no need to hunt for food or pelts. The competition between cattle and wild ruminants is also minimal. Disease, lack of attention, periodic flooding, screw worm infestations, predators, and harvesting tend to control herd size, preventing overgrazing or even optimal use of pastureland. It is common to see native fauna such as deer (four species), peccary (two species), tapir, and capybara grazing right along with range cattle. Most ranchers permit Sirionó to hunt on their land, increasing the territory available beyond the limits of Sirionó holdings. Some ranchers are particularly eager to have the Indians go after such predators as jaguars and puma, which kill calves, and it is commonly held by many mestizos in the region that the Indians are "naturally adept" at stalking and killing this type of prey.

While certain prejudices about the Sirionó may work in their favor, others do not. At least one rancher I met did not allow the Sirionó on his land because he said they "spooked" his cattle from their bad smell (an observation which I found totally unfounded) but he was one of those individuals who resented the Sirionó having land contiguous to his own. In spite of this injunction, the Sirionó continued to hunt on his property, merely waiting for the ranch owner to return to his home in Trinidad. They then gained permission from the *mayordomo* (overseer) to look for game. Most ranch workers are themselves indigenous people or descendants of mixed unions, making them more sympathetic toward the Sirionó and their need to hunt. As long as the cattle are not threatened, ranch personnel willingly look the other way. It is also common for Sirionó hunters to be given a place to stay on local ranches when they are on long hunts, and in return they will provide the ranch hands with some delicacy from a game animal they have killed.

Thus low population and a lack of competition for game resources, as well as compatibility among ruminants, have all contributed to successes for Sirionó hunters. But perhaps of even greater significance is the fact that the Sirionó are now mounted. This fact has had an impact on the group in several ways. First, and perhaps most obvious, the Sirionó can range farther afield, covering more territory and thus increasing their chances of finding game. Second, they can be more selective in the animals they hunt. "Trash" animals such as small birds and rodents taken in the past are ignored in the hope of finding something larger. Third, greater amounts of meat can be packed on animals and brought back to the village, lessening the frequency of hunts and also the likelihood of taking immature animals (except, as we saw, in the case of caimanes).

All of these factors help explain why Ibiato has remained a stable and viable community for more than fifty years, contradicting normal patterns and expectations. Some researchers, such as William Vickers, Daniel Gross, and Raymond Hames have found that resource depletion will force most Amazonian villagers to move to another site after twenty years or less of habitation. Still, Sirionó success rests on a precarious balance of circumstances. An increase in population, a shift from ranching to plow agriculture, or more sophisticated cattle management could alter the delicate equilibrium that has maintained Sirionó hunting for so many years. If hunting began to fail, they could theoretically become ranchers, since much of Sirionó land is savanna, but there has been little incentive to concentrate on cattle production while game remains plentiful.

As noted, the Sirionó focus on hunting as a meaningful and preferred way of life has made them less than diligent farmers. Most men and many women would rather spend their time in pursuit of game than clearing and working land. Part of the problem lies in the distance the Sirionó must travel to their chacos. In order to maintain vigilance over their holdings, the Sirionó no longer farm the land near the village but instead walk the ten kilometers to the parcel known as "La Esperanza" located on the other side of the lake. Before the road to El Carmen was begun, the lake had to be crossed by canoe, with pack animals swum across, a tedious and time-consuming chore. Now there is an earthen levee which can be traversed in much less time, but the trip still takes three hours or more. This alone discourages constant attention to agricultural activities. According to Anderson, even when farms were close to the village, the Sirionó had to be prodded into working them. During mission years, only two days out of six were alloted to hunting, the remainder to be devoted to farming. Now, there are no such constraints; consequently much more time is given to hunting or just relaxing in Ibiato than is to farming.

Most of the men in Ibiato clear only three or four *tareas* each year (a tarea is 10 by 100 meters). If they have selected a good area of virgin forest where the soil is "strong," they will harvest up to 90 *arrobas* (a measure of 25 pounds) of rice and about half that amount in corn that is planted at meter intervals among the young rice plants. When this crop is harvested, the land will be *carpido*, weeded, and then planted with manioc, plantains, and perhaps some sugarcane, papaya, or citrus trees. The virgin forest felled each year offers the advantage not only of being fertile but also of not requiring weeding before harvest. Once perennial crops such as plantains or sugarcane are established, they can survive with very little maintenance. The Sirionó chacos I visited were rather haphazardly cared for, especially in comparison to those of most lowlanders who live on their farms and are continually looking after their crops. The Sirionó have built small shelters on the land they farm and will remain in the chaco for several weeks at a time during the felling, burning, sowing, and harvesting seasons. But as soon as these chores are completed, the Sirionó return to their "town" homes in the village. A few of the older people, mainly those who lived much of their lives as nomads, remain in their chacos indefinitely, preferring the wilderness to life in Ibiato. Their continual presence on their small plots of land, however, seemed to have little effect on the condition of their fields, which were as unkempt as the rest.

Chiro told me that the previous planting season, September-November, several of the men had put in a hectare or even two in anticipation of the new road to Casarabe being improved and the one to Trinidad graveled. Their plan evidently was to try to market larger amounts of rice and to take advantage of the better prices offered in the city. Since both roads remained in poor condition from a lack of funding to continue the projects, getting these crops to market became impossible. In the past, farming in Ibiato has been done cooperatively since Anderson organized work teams with overseers to teach the Sirionó to farm. Today, as in the case of the men who put in a hectare or more of rice, work may also be done collectively, but it is not the norm. In spite of years of training to work in teams, Sirionó men would rather work individually. The complaints about collective work are typical of those expressed to me by other lowlands peasants: some men don't work well; others aren't *"cumplido"* (responsible); still others may not see the work through. One and a half hectares is not considered by most lowlanders to be an excessive amount of land to farm in any given year even with only one man working. The typical lowland peasant works one to two hectares himself, and up to five if he has help, again emphasizing the Sirionó lack of commitment to farming. It is normal to take two or perhaps three weeks at most to *rozar* (cut brush) and *tumbar* (fell trees) one hectare in preparation for burning. The Sirionó take one to two months to do the same work because they do not keep at it, taking time off to hunt or gather.

The exceptions to these patterns of work are the mestizo men living in Ibiato. One is Aiquiles Céspedes, the husband of Juana Eirubi, daughter of the ererecua Carlos Eirubi and half-sister to Chiro. Juana met Aiquiles in Trinidad, had a child by him while still married to Pablo Sosa, a half-Sirionó from Casarabe, and married Aiquiles after Pablo died. Aiquiles is a good Camba, lowlander, born in Trinidad but brought up in Santa Cruz. He spent a number of years wandering around the lowlands from one job to another and from one woman to another, finally ending up in the Beni with Juana. Aiquiles, like most of the other mestizo men in Ibiato, seems content but somehow out of place. He has been there longer than most, about five years, and is accepted and respected by the Sirionó. Still, he remains on the periphery of village life, spending most of his time with Chiro and other younger, more acculturated men. I had the impression that he and the other non-Sirionó men have sought some sort of refuge in Ibiato, a self-imposed exile from the more intense problems of the outside world. It is as if the time in Ibiato were simply a hiatus in their lives before deciding to return to the demands of daily existence in the larger context of Bolivian society. Most of the mestizo men in Ibiato eventually leave, tiring of its lack of activity or *"movimiento"* and of the "Indianness" of its residents. It is this latter point that underscores the perseverance of what is intrinsically Sirionó in the culture of the community. On the surface, Ibiato and its people appear no different from other peasant communities found in remote areas of the lowlands. They dress, cut their hair, and, except for very few of the older Sirionó who have not learned Spanish, talk like Benianos. In many respects, I found the Sirionó similar to people I knew in the Santa Cruz village of San Carlos where I lived and worked for four years as a Peace Corps volunteer. After a while, however, subtle differences begin to emerge. I suppose this might be termed the indigenous substrata, or their Sirionó culture that had never been totally suppressed or erased. I found this interesting—it was what I had come in hopes of finding. The mestizo men found it only strange and disquieting.

In the meantime, Aiquiles Céspedes continues to make his life in Ibiato, conforming to the norms of expected behavior. He drinks only rarely and attends church regularly although he was raised a Catholic. He is a good hunter and a hardworking farmer, planting at least one hectare of rice a year. Although Aiquiles seems to genuinely like the Sirionó, he like the other mestizos considers them poor and lazy farmers; consequently he is driven to outperform the Sirionó simply to show them what a "real" farmer can do. Aiquiles, however, does not walk ten kilometers to his chaco. He solicited and received land only four kilometers from the village and fenced it. Another reason the Sirionó work the land on the other side of the lake is that the town's cattle do not range there. As a result, Aiquiles spends one or two days a week working his land and tends his crops on a regular basis. Even so, his standard of living is about equal to that of the rest of the community; his house is small with few furnishings, and Juana dresses no better than the other women. They do have more money to spend on items such as sugar, lard, and coffee; but then, as a mestizo, Aiquiles is accustomed to three meals a day, not one or two, and to have rice on his plate rather than a roasted ear of corn, fruits, or palm nuts. Aiquiles, unlike the Sirionó, will store his rice and will look for the best price when he does sell it.

Most Sirionó sell their rice right in Ibiato, and consequently at low prices, to the *rescatadores* who scavenge small communities. Rescatadores are entrepreneurs with a little working capital that they invest in rice with the hope that the price will go up enough to give them a healthy profit. They search the most remote areas of the backlands, bringing along their own sacks and pack animals, and offer rock bottom prices to people who have little interest in making the long trip to Trinidad with a few arrobas of rice to sell. People like the Sirionó are likely to accept the offer of ready cash even though the price is far below market value. Normally, by three or four months after harvest, the Sirionó have consumed or sold all but the seed needed for next year's crop—and at times it goes as well. Another crop or two of corn will be planted for subsistence, with manioc, sweet potatoes, and plantains taking up the slack. In spite of their taste for and dependence on cultivated crops, the Sirionó still rely on wild foods periodically. Unlike mestizos who will eat these products as snack food, the Sirionó may spend days eating little else but motacú fruit, or aguaí, a large pear-like fruit which can be eaten raw or cooked. For the Sirionó these fruits are delicacies, and while they are in season, even rice, if it is available, will take a back seat.

In recent years, the Sirionó have begun receiving products from CARITAS, the Catholic Relief Service which distributes surplus food donated by the U.S. government. The villagers refer to these supplies as "los productos" and eagerly await their arrival every two months, assuming the road is passable and they can be brought from Trinidad. The products received include wheat and corn flour, CSM (corn-soy milk in powdered form), powdered cow's milk, and cooking oil. Having wheat flour means that bread can be baked, and for days on end the two big adobe ovens will be used almost continually. Although flour can be bought from time to time in Casarabe, it is always expensive. While I was in Ibiato, there was never any flour available in Casarabe's stores since the little that came in was hoarded by the mestizos for their own use and to bake bread for sale. Ibiato's young women have learned to bake well, and after weeks of a very monotonous diet, I too began to look forward to the arrival of "los productos" and the variety they offered.

In most respects, the Sirionó get along well on their own in terms of subsistence but they want to be able to purchase salt and sugar, having become accustomed to both after more than fifty years of use. There is no substitute for salt, which is usually obtained in the cheaper form of a block, mined in the highlands and shipped to the oriente. Sugar, however, is still somewhat of a luxury, since it can be replaced by honey or cane syrup. In precontact times, the Sirionó hunted for and consumed enormous quantities of wild honey. In fact, according to Silva, Anderson, and the older Sirionó, the major reason they wanted metal tools, particularly axes, was to be able to extract the honey from bee holes in trees more efficiently. Today, the Sirionó spend less time searching for honey than in the past; they produce sugarcane and can boil the juice into syrup.

For years the villagers had only a crude hand press consisting of a hole bored into a post with a long pole inserted to crush one section of cane at a time. Then in 1980, the people of Ibiato met and decided to hire a man in Casarabe who could make them a *trapiche*, a large geared press turned by horses or oxen. It cost 25,000 pesos in 1980, about U.S. $350. Two cows were sold and the remainder came from a head tax, or *cuota*, paid by every family. This was done without Jack's knowledge, and he was displeased to learn that he had not been consulted concerning the disposition of the town's cattle. Chiro was openly ambivalent about this issue when we talked about it, supporting the old missionary's desire to maintain the herd but also understanding the need for his people to provide more adequately for themselves. The trapiche took work and sacrifice to obtain and remains the pride and joy of the community.

Rather than have it built in Ibiato proper, the villagers placed the trapiche in the chacos where the sugarcane is readily accessible. Nancy, Chiro, some of the children, and I went out one day on horseback during my first visit in 1982 to give the press a try (it was still too early to harvest cane during my second trip). We cut the cane and pressed it rapidly, using the horses that we had ridden to drive the gears. The juice was cool and frothy and made a refreshing drink in the dry heat of the July day. We pressed more, enough to fill several containers we had brought along to take back to Ibiato to make syrup. After we returned to the village, Nancy boiled the liquid slowly for several hours, reducing it to a thick brown syrup which would keep for months. For many Sirionó, this is not only an acceptable substitute for white sugar (and certainly much more nutritious) but also for honey, which is harder to find and then not always in satisfactory amounts.

Interestingly, many of the Sirionó, or at least those taken by Perry Priest to Tumi Chuqua, have learned beekeeping. In spite of the fact that honey has always had a good market in Bolivia and would be an additional source of income, beekeeping among the Sirionó hasn't really caught on. Like farming, successful beekeeping requires almost constant attention and vigilance, something that the Sirionó do not want to be saddled with. To date, Chiro is the only Sirionó who keeps hives, working about six or eight. Since Chiro is no better a farmer than most, it may be that his devotion to beekeeping is more out of deference to his friendship with Perry. But then, given Chiro's level of acculturation, he may also perceive that if he sticks with it, he may reap some future profit as is the case with his cattle herd.

Perry Priest continues to support Chiro, or anyone else who might be interested in beekeeping, by providing hive bodies, wax foundation, and an extractor, which is kept in the Priests' house. Over the years, Chiro has become quite an experienced beekeeper, depending less on Perry's visits for advice. In recent years these visits have become more infrequent I was told; but according to Hernán Eato, one of the teachers, Perry and Anne were due for another shortly. Although the Priests had not spent the time in Ibiato that Anderson had, I knew their impact had been significant. Their presence in the village would no doubt offer new insights into the nature of the community.

TEN
Chapter 10

We learned of the imminent arrival of Perry and Anne Priest from the radio they had in their house. It was powered by a 12-volt car battery charged by a small solar unit nailed to a tall post outside. Hernán Eato would tend the radio once a week to see if there were any messages. One morning he was informed that the Priests would be flying in from Cochabamba in a week. When Nancy delivered this news to me I was certain there must have been some mistake. The airstrip was unusable. She responded by saying that the men would go out and patch it up, and, sure enough, the next morning Daniel and Arturo called the men to work. For the next four days a few of the men would take turns throwing dirt in the holes dug by pigs and cutting down brush. After they had finished I walked the length of the strip. It still looked like a death trap. It had been raining almost every day, and the dirt covering the holes had only soaked up the rainwater and turned to mud.

The morning of the Priests' arrival was partly cloudy with rain not far off. I wondered if they would cancel the flight. At 10 a.m. Hernán turned on the radio for the latest bulletin. The Priests were on their way. Shortly before noon a small plane flew over the village, banking sharply to the south in preparation for landing. We all ran down to the airstrip to meet the visitors. I still found it inconceivable that anyone would attempt anything but an emergency landing on the field. Images of a plane catapulting end over end flashed through my mind as I watched the craft coming down near the treetops. The Sirionó were smiling and talking loudly, trying to mask their obvious concern over what was about to happen. I walked over to Chiro and Nancy. Chiro looked solemn. "Will they make it?" I asked. "I think so. The mission pilots are good at this sort of thing," Chiro said.

The plane was headed straight in now, the motor barely audible as the pilot throttled back and lowered the flaps. When they touched down there was a huge spray of mud that partially obliterated our view. The pilot fought his craft as it plunged in and out of potholes and skated back and forth across the slick field. After what seemed hours the plane finally came to a halt at the far end of the airstrip. The entire fuselage and the undersides of the wings were covered with dripping, black ooze.

The pilot taxied the plane up the field toward the throng of people waiting there. The Priests climbed out, looking pale and shaken. Their grim faces quickly turned to smiles as the Sirionó rushed in to greet them. Both Perry and Anne looked at me briefly a few times, obviously not remembering me and for an instant showing a frown of concern as they rapidly tried to assess who I might be and what I was doing in Ibiato. I took that moment to approach them and introduce myself. At the mention of Gainesville, Perry remembered me, and again there was that quick flash of assessment. They were warm in their greeting, but I had a momentary feeling that I was seen as an intruder in this domain that had been the source of their efforts for so many years.

The Priests' few supplies for their two-week stay were unloaded and carried up to their house. I dropped out of the crowd to say hello to the pilot and to express concern about the condition of the field. He told me that it was one of the worst he had seen in a long time and that if it didn't dry out in the next two weeks, the Priests would have to get to Trinidad by land where he would pick them up. Then he asked me if he could bring me anything if he made the return trip. I demurred.

The pilot repeated his offer, and again I refused. He looked at me oddly. I told him that I was an anthropologist, apropos of nothing. I suppose I wanted to test his sincerity. I knew that once I delivered this information, he would probably be less inclined to offer assistance. Anthropologists and SIL missionaries have a long history of mutual antagonism. He smiled and asked about the type of work I was doing and if I had found "anything interesting." I relaxed a little. We talked a few more minutes and then he went to the Priests' house, no doubt to discuss the return trip.

An hour later the pilot walked back to his plane to prepare for the flight to Cochabamba. After checking everything, he had the men roll the airplane as far back off the end of the strip as possible, gaining every inch available. With the brakes set, he pushed the throttle wide open. The wings and fuselage began to vibrate violently. When it seemed as if the plane would tear itself apart, the pilot released the brakes and the plane began to move forward. At that moment, he pulled up the nose, using a maneuver I had never seen before. The plane sped down the field on just the two rear wheels, which would reduce the chance of its flipping over should it hit a deep hole. With a tremendous roar and a spray of mud, the plane lifted off the field, circling back over the village before heading west toward Cochabamba.

The Priests spent their first few days in Ibiato making their house livable again. It had been many months since their last visit and the place needed repairs: a new fence around the small porch to keep out the cattle that liked to sleep there at night—the same cows that kept me awake when I had stayed in the house; some adobe in a large hole in a side wall where the pigs had rooted; and a few new tiles to replace the ones that had cracked from the falling limbs of the huge tamarind tree that shaded the house. During this time, I kept my distance, still wary of these new arrivals and concerned how I would be treated by them. As the days passed, I would walk by their house on my way to Nancy's, always greeting them but still remaining aloof. If there was a strategy to this, I suppose it was to avoid any interaction that could put me in an adversarial position with the Priests. Nancy was a little curious why I didn't seek out these people who were her friends and my countrymen, and I really didn't have an answer that would make sense to her.

Then, after lunch one day Nancy and I were working on a hammock in her house. The Priests had brought in a Guarayo woman several years ago to teach the women how to weave cotton hammocks using a homemade loom. Several of the Sirionó women still practiced this art, and when thread was available they would make hammocks that could be sold in Trinidad. Anne Priest usually brought thread with her from Cochabamba and would sell it to the women at cost. Nancy had purchased enough to make a large hammock for Chiro, taking the time to instruct me in the different designs they used. There was a knock at the door and Anne Priest walked in. Nancy was a little shy, as she always is around visitors and especially those she perceives as being of higher social status. Anne sat down and began to chat with us. She was cheerful and pleasant, but I had a hard time moving freely into the conversation. Then she asked Nancy if she would "let me go" for the evening so I might have supper with them. Nancy replied that she hadn't planned anything special for dinner that night. It was a neat trick. At first I was resentful at having been so deftly maneuvered into a social occasion with the Priests, especially since I suspected that it would turn into an evening of Bible recitations and earnest efforts to effect my conversion. Finally, I realized that my past experiences with fundamentalist missionaries in the field had led to stereotyping and subsequent avoidance behavior. Not only had I not given the Priests a fair chance, I had compromised my objectivity. From a professional standpoint, my reluctance to interact with them was also serving to restrict access to information necessary to my research.

At dinner that night I opened the conversation by asking Perry why the Sirionó called him "Taita Eoco." He told me that his given name is almost impossible to pronounce and there is no Spanish equivalent. Thus the Sirionó gave him a nickname according to their custom, which is to choose some outstanding physical characteristic. Since Perry is well over six feet tall, the Sirionó call him Long-tall Elder. Anne, whose name has a Spanish counterpart, is simply referred to as Señora Ana. I judged the Priests to be in their middle to late fifties. They had worked in Bolivia most of their adult lives, dividing their time at first between San Pedro de Richards, Tumi Chuqua, and, later, Ibiato, translating the New Testament into Sirionó, a task that took twenty-five years. During that time, several informants, including Chiro, where taken to Tumi Chuqua to help with the work and also to receive instruction in Christianity. In recent years, Perry had been named the SIL director for Bolivia, but the program was now being phased out. Tumi Chuqua had been turned over to the Bolivian government, and the Priests would be leaving the country in a matter of months. These two weeks, they explained, were part of their annual leave and they had elected to spend them with the Sirionó in Ibiato.

When I questioned the Priests more closely about the nature of their work, they carefully avoided the religious aspects. Although SIL is a mission group, the field branch of Wycliffe Bible Translators, its influence and longevity in many nations are largely due to concerted efforts by its members to present themselves as linguists, not missionaries. By and large, SIL missionaries are better educated and somewhat more liberal in their views toward existing traditions than other groups. Unlike many other fundamentalist missions, SIL is willing to make certain accommodations with native peoples, claiming to work within native cultural contexts. Still, it would appear that their effects on indigenous peoples have been uneven, causing alarm and criticism from protectionist organizations such as Survival International.

After this first meeting, I spent additional time with the Priests, visiting with them on their porch along with any Sirionó who happened by. Both Anne and Perry speak fluent Sirionó and, unless they are with those who never learned it, will insist on using only Sirionó. (Nancy, like several others, cannot speak Sirionó. She was brought up on a ranch north of Ibiato where her mother was the only Sirionó speaker.) Perry is very much a proponent of seeing the Sirionó language preserved and has been instrumental in keeping Spanish only a second language in the community. Much of his influence has come through the schooling of the children who receive bilingual education until the fourth grade. Two of the three Sirionó bilingual teachers were trained at Tumi Chuqua.

Perry has been able to achieve state-sanctioned, bilingual education in Ibiato because of the influence SIL has in Bolivia's Ministry of Education. With expertise needed in areas of indigenous instruction that Bolivian educators could not supply, SIL linguists were able to establish a firm niche in this administrative sector. With this leverage, they could, of course, see that many of their own converts and trainees were given teaching positions throughout the country. From one vantage point, it became an effective means of infiltrating a public system with individuals bent on proselytizing their particular ideology. But from another it also insured that the Sirionó as well as other indigenous groups would have their own teachers and that native languages would be taught in school. In order for this to occur, all of the materials used by the bilingual teachers had to be prepared and printed by SIL, with the approval of the Ministry of Education. These teaching aids, however, are secular in nature and many of them focus on themes of traditional Sirionó culture.

The village of Ibiato receives government salaries for four teachers: three are Sirionó and one is a "fiscal," sent from Trinidad. Given the paucity of Bolivia's resources, it is highly unusual for a village with only seventy school-age children to have four full-time teachers. Again, this can only be attributed to Perry's influence with the ministry. Before the Priests arrived on this latest visit to Ibiato, word was sent from the Ministry of Education office in Trinidad that two of the *items* were to be discontinued, those salaries held by Hernán Eato and Eddy Ino, both trained in bilingual education at Tumi Chuqua. The reason given for releasing these lines was that neither man had attended a state normal school and so was not properly certified. The third Sirionó teacher, Nataniel Jacinto, had been sent by Perry to the normal school in Riberalta when it opened and so holds a legitimate teaching certificate. When it seemed as if Ibiato would indeed lose two of its teachers, Perry arrived to say that the problem had been "worked out." Both Hernán and Eddy were on the payroll when the school year began.

Although Nataniel is much younger than Hernán and Eddy, his status as a "normalista" has given him greater respect than his age might normally merit. He is the appointed director of the school and keeps all the records. Nata, as he is known, is also a skilled hunter, adding to his status as respected teacher. The salaries received by the *Maestros rurales* (rural teachers) are very low, usually no more than US $20-25 a month, when they are paid (lately a sporadic process). As a consequence, quality and motivation among rural teachers tend to be low, and Eddy and Hernán can both be so described, a fact that is recognized by the villagers who frequently grumble about the two men's lack of interest in their work. Nata, on the other hand, not only has received probably better training but is young and enthusiastic, taking his job as a teacher seriously. His efforts have paid off in the praise he receives from students and parents.

Although the three teachers receive the only salaries in the community, their pay is not enough to set them above the others. In fact, because Eddy and Hernán not only are poor teachers but poor hunters as well, preferring instead to buy meat from others when they have money, their positions as schoolteachers have failed to give them any additional prestige in the village.

Being of a chiefly line, Nataniel is the only one of the three teachers who could at some point vie for the position of ererecua. He, like Chiro, is well educated and highly acculturated, but his youth (he is twenty-four) precludes much real decision-making at present. Nata likes to listen to his big stereo radio, play soccer, and teach school. For the moment, he gives no indication of seeking power or threatening the existing authority of Daniel and Arturo. The villagers perceive him as a competent teacher but not yet someone to be reckoned with.

The fourth teacher is always an outsider and always a problem. None has lasted more than one school year, and several haven't made it more than a few weeks. Again, it is the issue of placing a mestizo, albeit from a rural background, in an Indian community. The complaints from both sides are always the same. The mestizo teacher invariably tries to seduce his female students or the wives of the men; in the one or two instances where the teacher was a woman, the same held true. And, particularly in the case of the male teachers, there is the drinking problem. It would appear that as the situation in Ibiato becomes more difficult for them and hostilities arise, the teachers drink more often and to greater excess. At that point, they are asked to leave and a replacement requested.

From the teachers' side, they expect adequate accommodations during their tenure in any village. The Sirionó's ideas about adequate housing and a mestizo's are usually quite disparate. The teacher who arrived during my stay and who was to have taught fifth and sixth grades was given space in the Anderson house. The Sirionó began construction of a separate dwelling, but the men were unenthusiastic about completing it. The teacher tired of the bats and lack of privacy and left after one week. He was also to have been supplied with meat, but no one could decide whose turn it was to do this. His disgust was apparent when he loaded his few belongings on a borrowed horse and rode to Casarabe. In spite of Ibiato's reputation as an undesirable post, the government continues to provide fiscal teachers each year. This too can be attributed to Perry's influence at higher levels in the Ministry of Education.

There are six grades taught in the brick and tile schoolhouse built by Anderson many years ago. When Jack was in the village, he paid to have teachers work there since the government at that time was not willing to invest its resources in an Indian mission. Perry Priest changed that when he took his work to Ibiato. The present system is set up so that Hernán and Eddy teach the lower grades, and these mostly in Sirionó. Nata takes the third and fourth grades which are taught in Sirionó and Spanish, and the outside teacher has the two upper grades, both in Spanish only. Every child in Ibiato attends school, the importance of which was stressed first by Anderson and later by the Priests. Parents living in the outlying areas send their children to Ibiato to live with relatives and attend school, or they actually move the family to the village during the term. Even older children, fourteen or fifteen years of age, may continue to attend classes simply because there is so little else to do.

When the school year finally began in 1984 after several prolonged national strikes, the children were eager to go to class. Although their clothing may be stained and mended, they are sent to school in clean clothes and with combed hair. I watched to see if these efforts at appearance would begin to falter, as is frequently the case in small villages once the newness of school wears off, but it did not. Getting ready to go to school each day was a frenzied hour of dressing and getting hair braided or slicked down, collecting a pencil and notebook (purchased from Don Adolfo), and finding a stool or chair to take along to sit on. Education is taken very seriously in Ibiato.

School in Ibiato, like most rural villages in Bolivia, is a makeshift affair in spite of the formality with which education is viewed. There are no books other than the three or four owned by teachers, and the only classroom equipment other than a few old desks consists of a painted piece of plywood used as a chalkboard. The school receives one box of chalk a year that Nata carefully hoards, handing out only what is absolutely necessary. Most of the learning involves rote memorization—copying down lessons from the blackboard and then reciting them from memory. A great deal of time is spent in repeating these lessons aloud, and as I passed by the school I would laugh at how the children's high voices sounded just like the creek frogs singing in unison. In spite of these obstacles, the students do learn to read and write, and in two languages. I remember the young people I knew in San Carlos who, after five or six years in school, soon lost their literacy for simple lack of practice. In Ibiato, however, all but the old and recent arrivals can read, and read well. Once out of school, most of their reinforcement comes from reading the Bible. In contrast to mestizo communities that are predominately Catholic, the people of Ibiato read their Bibles frequently. Bibles are rare in Catholic towns since Catholicism has never stressed their use. If people do own them, most are incapable of making out more than a few simple words because of the infrequency of use. In light of my previous experience in Catholic villages, I found it more than a little strange to be in a predominately Protestant community surrounded by people who routinely sat around and read their Bibles.

In spite of his past involvement in the religious formation of the community, Perry kept a low profile in this area. I had to wonder if some of this was due to my being there. However, his wife, Anne, took a dominant role in the religious life of the village. Whether this was thrust upon her as a last-minute accommodation to the presence of an anthropologist, I have no idea; but it certainly gave Anne the lion's share of work. In addition to teaching a week long "Vacation Bible School" for the children in which they learned hymns and Bible passages in Sirionó, Anne, a registered nurse, tended the sick from the front room of their small home. While this was going on, Perry puttered around the house and had a few apparently intense counseling sessions with several of the village men. One of these was Raúl, also a onetime student at Tumi Chuqua. Raúl had been drinking steadily for months, depriving his family of necessities, abusing his wife, and generally making a nuisance of himself. He spent several afternooons with Perry on the porch, huddled over in earnest conversation. I could only guess at the content of these discussions; but the following Sunday Raúl got up in church and with eyes brimming over, begged forgiveness of everyone for his past behavior, promising to reform his ways. I thought the entire episode humiliating. When I looked around, however, I realized I was the only one in the congregation with any misgivings. Raúl had slowly been alienating himself from the community. The confession of guilt may have been couched in religious terms, but it was more a public expression of social transgressions. When it was over, there was thunderous applause and Raúl was welcomed back into the community, forgiven and a new man.

On their second and last Sunday in Ibiato, the Priests played an active role in the morning's service. Perry was careful in explaining to me beforehand that the people had asked him to preach, and that he was only complying with their wishes because he and his wife would be leaving soon. Perry delivered the sermon in Sirionó, and after the service, Anne had her Bible school students present the hymns and passages they had learned. John 3:16 was popular this year. The recital delighted the Sirionó who enjoyed watching their offspring show off what they had learned.

For many Sirionó, I suspect attendance at church on Sundays and weeknights is more an act of *comunitas* than faith. In spite of years of teaching, Christianity seems to have layered over, rather than replaced, earlier animistic beliefs. The Sirionó consider themselves *creyentes* (true believers, as opposed to Catholics who are not); but from a purely fundamentalist perspective, they retain many "superstitions." Christianity for the Sirionó is a new set of beliefs and ideas, many of which they cannot relate to in terms of their specific situation. It seems to work best in the church on the mound, in the cleared space connected to the outside world by trails and roads and radio waves. It also works very well in the big church in Trinidad that Anderson built and where he still preaches every night and most of the day on Sunday. But once the Sirionó move outside the civilization that fits so well with its Christian ideologies, things are different. In the wilderness God still exists, but now there are also other beings: strange, unexplainable, malevolent spirits that inhabit the recesses of the forest. The Sirionó drift back and forth between these two worlds easily, never questioning whether one ideology might conflict with the other. They are both necessary and useful. Even the most acculturated Sirionó like Chiro, Vicente, and Nathaniel still pay heed to the mysteries of the wilderness.

One evening we were sitting at the small table finishing our supper of masaco and tea when we heard a loud crash from the woods nearby. Chiro's house is located at the base of the mound, close to the wooded *arroyo* that flows around it. Much of the creek becomes a tangled swamp during the rainy season. Again, there was a thrashing sound. We stopped eating and listened carefully. I said it sounded like a cow. Chiro shook his head no, cattle never went into that area—it was too thick and mucky. Maybe it was an *anta*, a tapir. Chiro got out his flashlight and .22 and then called to Wilson, Nancy's brother, who lived only a few yards away. Wilson, too, had heard the sound, and met Chiro half way. He was joined by his wife, Doroty, some of their older children, Nancy's mother, Elena, and stepfather, Demetrio. Our group walked silently toward the low spot where the noise seemed to be coming from. A few more people, Eddy Ino, his wife, Asunta, and Pedro Pepe caught up with us. The talk was hushed and speculative as Chiro and Wilson worked their way into the tangle. Every now and then the thrashing could be heard. Nancy and Demetrio told me it must be something bad, a jaguar but not a jaguar. An evil spirit in the form of the tiger. Or even a sorcerer who had taken the form of a jaguar. At this an older man, Julio Bei, approached to agree with the latter suggestion.

"A few years ago," he said, "I went hunting with a Guarayo. Everyone told me not to hunt with him because he was a brujo. But I decided to go anyway. When we were well into the forest, he turned and told me, 'Don't be afraid at what you are going to see. Don't run away.' Then he walked on ahead and before I knew it there was a tiger standing there. The tiger went off into the forest, returning shortly with a *taitetú* [collared peccary] it had killed. It left the taitetú and returned to the woods. The Guarayo came out. He walked over to the animal, picked it up and motioned for me to come along. I never went hunting with that man again."

Julio Bei's story was met with knowing looks from the members of the slowly increasing gallery of onlookers. Finally, Chiro and Wilson came crawling back up a fallen tree trunk they had used as a pathway into the swamp. All they could see, Chiro said, was some reddish fur.

"It's the tiger!" whispered Demetrio. Fear seemed to grip the onlookers. "Kill it! Shoot it now before it gets anyone!"

"No," Chiro said, "The fur doesn't look right to be a jaguar. I want to try to get a better look."

Two of the younger men joined Chiro and Wilson as they tried to clear away some of the undergrowth and heavy vines. Then one of the men shouted that it was a cow. It had mired itself in the swamp and became so entangled it was immobilized. But rather than calm people's fear, this news only seemed to increase it.

"It's not a real cow. Cows never go in there," one woman said, repeating Chiro's earlier pronouncement. "It must be a brujo."

The men brought machetes, axes, and lassos and, after about twenty minutes' work, extricated the animal. I had to admit that the poor cow, covered with mud and wild-eyed from fear, looked like an apparition. Once freed, it raised its tail and ran down the trail into the forest. "I knew it!" said Demetrio. "It's not a cow. No cow would head into the woods alone on a dark night like tonight. It would join the others in the village!"

There were murmurs from the crowd. Slowly, people began to return to their homes, but there was concern in their voices as they quietly talked among themselves. Nancy, Chiro, the children, and I went back to the house as well. The in-laws and a few neighbors congregated in the room while we finished our now cold supper. After we had eaten, Chiro told this story:

"When I was about 19, I went on an *ito* [long hunt] with several people including my grandfather's brother. At the *pascana* [camp] the women made chicha from palm heart and honey, and let it stand for a few days. Then the men got drunk. My grandfather's brother got very drunk and sick. He would go off for a while and then return. Then he got into his string hammock. At that moment a strange sound was heard in the forest, a whistling wind. It came closer and closer and then swirled through camp, upsetting everything and frightening everyone. Even the dogs were barking furiously. When the wind left, the people noticed that the old man in the hammock was breathing strangely—then he stopped breathing entirely. People were very frightened. When dawn came they dug a shallow grave as quickly as possible. At this time they noticed that all the *patujuces* [a broad-leafed plant that grows in low areas] near our camp had been flattened down, and that the old man's tracks were everywhere. It was as if something had dragged him around in there. Another man and I were the last to leave the place because we had to look for our dogs that had run off after some pigs. As we were coming through the forest we heard several cries. Ai...ai...ai....I thought perhaps my grandfather's brother wasn't dead after all and was coming back to life. I tried to persuade the others to go back and see, but no one would come with me. No one has ever gone back to that place."

Others that night told similar stories of the unknown, linking death, sickness, and bad luck with the evil woods spirits. Interestingly, these malevolent beings were never equated with Satan or his messengers, a frequent practice among people who have received teachings in Christianity.

For the Sirionó, the world of the forest is something very distinct from that outside, two separate domains of experience. The old ways and beliefs must be respected and heeded if one is to survive in the wilderness; but in the day-to-day struggle of being modern Bolivians as well, Christianity is the Sirionó's passport to move among those who make the rules. In many ways, the duality of their beliefs is a metaphor for life as a whole. The Sirionó straddle the old and the new and must be able to function in both.

Just as the Sirionó move deftly from one set of religious beliefs to another, they also manage to juggle traditional with contemporary concepts of sickness and health. Because the Sirionó had no shamans or other religious specialists, the introduction of modern medical practices did not create any conflicts of interest as it has among the Guarayos. The Sirionó readily make use of modern pharmaceuticals if they are available, particularly antibiotics and vaccines. They will also seek hospitalization in Trinidad in the case of serious illness or accident. In an effort to have health care available in Ibiato, Nancy and some of the other women had been attending classes in Trinidad to be trained as village health specialists. The government pays for the instruction, room, and board of the participants during the one week of classes held four times in the course of a year. When the women have completed this training, one of them will receive a small salary and a supply of medicines. In the meantime, Anne Priest supplemented this instruction by working with them and anyone else interested in learning how to deal with injury, sickness, and childbirth.

At first glance, it would appear that the Sirionó have become completely modernized in their concepts of medicine and illness, but their ready acceptance of Western practices can be somewhat misleading. Operating on another level are the folk beliefs that Sirionó continue to hold. In most instances, the two systems do not come into conflict. If modern medicine is available, old methods and beliefs will be set aside. The Sirionó are well aware that it is more effective. The one exception to this is witchcraft, which is not native to the Sirionó but is greatly feared by them. This was the case with the baby who died from pneumonia after the mother gave in to the bruja and witchcraft won out over modern medicine. It was not that the child's mother preferred witchcraft but that pressure put on her by the bruja was too much to withstand. Had the child survived, the incident would have given the sorceress a stronger foothold in the community and a potential source of income.

Unlike their traditional animistic beliefs that exist outside of Christianity, the Sirionó equate witchcraft with the forces of evil, or Satan. Brujos have crossed that boundary between nature and civilization, placing them in opposition to those beliefs that operate in the modern world. It is trespassing and therefore dangerous, threatening the equilibrium the villagers have established between their two worlds. Several Guarayos have been literally run out of town for practicing witchcraft. One, a young male, was stripped and publicly whipped by the ererecuas before being escorted to the trail out of the village. The Sirionó bruja from Salvatierra who was now residing in the community presented a different sort of problem—she was one of their own. Still, she received a formal visit and a stern warning from the two ererecuas as well as one from Chiro and Vicente to cease her activities or face expulsion from Ibiato.

There is also distinction now made between brujos, or sorcerers, and curanderos, or healers, a difference most probably learned from other peasant peoples in the area. Again, because the Sirionó had no tradition of shamanism, they do not have specialists adept at curing practices. This knowledge, which remains rudimentary at best, is shared by all. The closest the Sirionó have to a real curandero is Pastor Mateo Pópole who is actually a partero (male midwife), something very rare in the lowlands or anywhere for that matter. Since men were never excluded from witnessing childbirth (although women traditionally handled deliveries), the Sirionó see nothing strange or improper in having a male in this role. Pastor explained that he had little choice but to assist his wife in her deliveries since they were alone for so many years on a ranch with only males in residence. As each child came along, he learned a little more, eventually being called to other ranches to help with deliveries. Over time, he became very skilled at his craft, having remarkable success in diagnosing potential complications and accurately assessing fetal position by external palpation. He also experimented with externally manipulating the fetus to avoid breech presentations. Now, people as far away as Casarabe will seek out his aid in a difficult birth. He is credited with a great many successful deliveries of difficult cases and with having saved numerous lives. As his fame spread, his fees got higher so that now only those with adequate resources can afford his prenatal care. Pastor has never refused an emergency summons, however, and will come at any hour to attend someone in need of his services.

Most births in Ibiato occur without complication and are attended by one or two of the older women or a few of the younger. Today, the Sirionó are aware of the hazards of infection and will be careful to use only a sterile knife or razor when cutting the umbilical cord. During the first years of contact, many infants were lost to tetanus infections because steel knives began to replace the bamboo sliver customarily used for this purpose. The bamboo cutting blade was always taken directly from a growing stalk and was clean because it had to be peeled. Once knives became common, they would just be picked up off the ground and used. Now, the Sirionó understand the connection between tetanus and unclean objects and so are careful in what they use to sever the umbilical cord. As a consequence, the number of children are increasing, and, once vaccinated against common childhood diseases, they have a better chance of surviving to maturity than in the past.

Many of the old beliefs concerning sickness and health that have persisted are based on a simple transference of the physical characteristics of plant and animal foods to people, particularly pregnant women. Thus a pregnant woman should not eat double fruits or she will have twins (usually smaller at birth and therefore more likely to die); she should not consume animals with "turned" feet such as anteaters or sloths or she will have a club-footed child; deformed animals should not be eaten because they cause deformed children; turtle eggs are also taboo—they are covered with a membrane and this bears a resemblance to a woman's womb when it extrudes. Intestines are another forbidden food item because they cause the cord to wrap around the infant's neck. Neither should a woman eat from the sides of the rice pot where the grain was stuck since it will cause the placenta to remain attached after birth. Children should not eat ears of corn with worms in them because their teeth will rot.

While these taboos are known by even the younger girls, they are seldom observed with any regularity. The older women may exert some pressure to do so if they are in residence with a daughter or daughter-in-law, but there is a tendency now to ignore these restrictions. Still, when a child is born with a deformity such as a clubfoot, there will be talk that it was because the mother ate an anteater or a sloth.

Perhaps because many of these old beliefs don't come into direct conflict with Christianity, the Priests have not preached against them. There seems to be a recognition that they belong to a "folk tradition" that is basically innocuous and, at times, even worth preserving. Some of Perry's linguistic work has entailed the transcription and publication of Sirionó customs and the old tales related by Jêjê and others. Unlike other fundamentalist missionaries I have encountered, the Priests seem to value much of what is Sirionó culture and are concerned with its survival. Needless to say, they also wish to have someone around to read the New Testament translation that took them a quarter of a century to complete.

The weather improved enough during the Priests' two-week stay for the plane to return. It was another rough landing, but not as bad as the first. The pilot climbed out of the cockpit, reached into his pocket, and with a grin handed me an enormous Swiss chocolate bar. I had the wrapper off and was savoring my first bite when the small plane lifted off and droned into the distance.

ELEVEN
Chapter 11

It didn't take very long for Ibiato's company manners to wear off. After the Priests left, things pretty much settled back to normal. While the missionary couple was in Ibiato people were on their best behavior—no drinking and no squabbling. There had been a similar reaction at first to my presence in the village; but once the Sirionó realized I wasn't a missionary and wasn't there to oversee their behavior, life went on as usual.

Ibiato is in many respects an idyllic place. The location is marvelously picturesque, with its towering mound and tidy thatched houses spread among glossy green citrus trees. The ground is carpeted with grass kept short by the cows that quietly graze there. Above it all stands the church, now in disrepair but still a proud sentinel overlooking the community. Most of the days in Ibiato are quiet, its residents going about their chores in a kind of monotonous harmony. Days may go by without any clear distinction between them, making time seem almost nonexistent. Nestled on top of the mound and surrounded by the endless expanse of forest and pampa, Ibiato often seemed alone in the universe, the true center of nature and reality itself, as indeed it is for the Sirionó who live there.

This harmony and tranquility are disrupted on occasion by tragedy and dissent. The Sirionó struggle constantly against the misfortunes of illness, accidents, death, and the petty and not so petty disagreements they hatch among themselves. In this, then, the Sirionó of today are faced with resolving the same day-to-day conflicts and internecine strife that confronted the isolated, homogeneous bands of their forebears. Like their relatives of the past, the Sirionó expend a considerable amount of time in disputes over women, men, and their relationships with each other.

In precontact times, the better hunters and more important ererecuas had the right to more than one spouse. Today, that custom no longer exists although both men and women may engage in serial monogmy, the successive acquisition of mates. One custom that does persist is the sharing of partners, or what in modern usage is termed spouse-swapping. In the old days, it was common for brothers to share the sexual favors of their wives; and on occasion, even close friends might do the same. Although this was a male prerogative (women who on their own sought extramarital sexual relationships would, if caught, be punished by exclusion from the conjugal hammock for a day or two), the women frequently enjoyed variety as well. This practice certainly has not been condoned by either of Ibiato's missionaries, but in the way of cultural persistence it continues among many of the people. The Sirionó refer to the custom of spouse swapping as *repasando,* a Spanish word meaning literally "to pass back and forth." I had never heard of either the practice or the terminology among lowlands mestizos. Later, I presented the question to two older Camba friends in Santa Cruz, one of whom had spent many years in the Beni. Neither had ever heard of the custom or the term. Thus I had to conclude that the Sirionó coined this word themselves.

Normally, repasando is a casual alliance, one that occurs sporadically and then only lasts a night or two. During my stay in Ibiato, however, the swapping between two pairs of partners became serious, resulting in one pair wanting to remain together while the other wanted to return to their spouses. This disagreement quickly became public, requiring the involvement of both of the ererecuas and the two pastors.

The tendency of the village leaders, both religious and secular, is to ignore people's private lives. Only when minor disputes become public scandals are they inclined to interfere. I thought it interesting that the missionaries had no such inhibitions but that their Sirionó protégés refrained from imposing moral judgments unless public opinion forced them into it. Daniel, Arturo, Chiro, and Vicente took turns visiting and counseling the four individuals involved in the repasando case. Although all four leaders chastised the couples in terms of moral principles of right and wrong, their primary concern was the stability of the community. This problem was initiating open commentary and families were beginning to take sides, always a serious consequence of any dispute. Since virtually everyone in Ibiato is related through ties of blood or marriage, disagreements have the potential of dividing the community. Thus the concern of all the leaders is to preserve unity, and if the issue requires concessions and compromises to reach a peaceful agreement, religious ideology may have to be laid aside temporarily. The loyalty of the Sirionó is first to themselves and then to their religion. Although the ererecuas and pastors would have preferred to resolve the repasando case by having the partners return to their original status, this was not going to happen. The couple was allowed to remain together, their spouses were given a small property settlement, and tempers finally cooled.

As was apparent from the repasando incident, relationships between Sirionó women and men can be quite fluid. Although the missionaries have attempted to instill the idea of the sanctity and permanency of the marital union, the Sirionó treat these bonds rather casually. Typically during their young adult lives, women and men will have a series of spouses, ultimately settling down into a more or less permanent relationship. It is also common for men and women to seek sexual relationships outside of a present union. The frequency of these "affairs" makes excellent grist for the gossip mills, the primary source of entertainment in Ibiato. If these casual affairs should become serious, the pair will usually leave the village for a while, moving out to the chacos or taking a job on a ranch. Once the furor has died down, they will return to Ibiato and reestablish residence. These upheavals in social relationships keep the village leaders busy carrying out shuttle diplomacy among the individuals and families involved.

Nancy and some of her age-mates like Juana Eirubi, Petrona Jicarere, and the two sisters Mereya and Lila Suárez always kept abreast of the current status of particular relationships in the village and were eager to share these bits of gossip with each other and with me. Women like these play an important role in matchmaking, although it is an indirect one. Mostly, they pass information between adolescent boys and girls, letting each know of the intents and interests of the other. If there is a general consensus among several of the women that a particular relationship would be a good match, encouragement, and at times even pressure, is put on the pair to begin to cohabit, living at first either with the boy's or girl's family. In this way the teacher, Nataniel, was encouraged by Juana Eirubi and her friends to marry Dalia, Juana's daughter.

Sometimes a young couple will be very discreet in their attraction for one another, and no one really is aware of the relationship until they run off together to live with a relative in the chacos or an understanding friend in the village. At times there are also courtships that do not meet with the approval of one or both of the respective families. The girl may be beaten by her mother to discourage any further involvement, but it is usually ineffective. The couple will simply elope, leaving Ibiato to work on a ranch or perhaps move to Trinidad for a time. After a while they too will return, the families by then having reconciled themselves to the match.

Nancy's marriage to Chiro fell into this latter category. She and Chiro had one of the more stable unions in the village so I was surprised to learn of its rocky beginnings.

CHAPTER ELEVEN

When Chiro was in his early twenties, he lived for a while with a Guarayo woman and had a son by her. For about five years there had been a settlement of Guarayos near Ibiato and some intermarriage had taken place. But the Sirionó and Guarayo did not get along well together. The Sirionó were constantly accusing the Guarayos of thievery and drunkenness. There were also several violent incidents, including the killing of a Sirionó by a Guarayo during a drinking bout. Then too, there was the ever present problem of witchcraft. The group was finally forced out by Anderson and the Sirionó themselves. Chiro's spouse left as well, leaving him with his young son, William. Nancy at that time was about sixteen and had had her eye on Chiro for quite a while. As she explained: "Agustín Eatandu wanted me. He kept coming around the house, talking to my mother and bringing her meat. Then my mother took me to the chaco with Agustín. She wanted me to sleep with him. But I didn't want to, so I ran away and came back to Ibiato to be with Don Nancho and his wife. (Nancho Justiniano and his wife were teachers hired by the Andersons who lived in Ibiato for a number of years after the Andersons left.) They took me in and gave me shelter. My mother and Agustín talked the two ererecuas into going to Don Nancho and asking him to give me to Agustín. Don Nancho asked me if I wanted to go with him and I said no. He kept them from taking me. I loved Chiro and not Agustín. One day, while my mother was in the chaco, Chiro came and took me to his house. My mother didn't want me to be with Chiro because he had lived with a Guarayo and had her child. He also didn't bring my mother gifts. When my mother returned from the chaco and saw I was with Chiro she was very angry. Agustín was also mad at first too, but he married Petrona and we are all friends now. My mother accepted Chiro and loves him very much. She sat down with me and advised me to be a good wife and to serve my husband well."

When the women and I talked of marriage and courting behavior, I also questioned them about preferred marriage partners. During Holmberg's research, the Sirionó evidently engaged in what is known as cross-cousin marriage, or the preference of one's mother's brother's offspring or father's sister's child as a potential spouse. Try as I might, I could neither find evidence that this occurred in the past or that it was going on at present. When I offered the kinship term "yande," I was given the correct response that it meant potential spouse. However, when I attempted to link this term with a cross-cousin, I was simply told repeatedly, "We don't marry cousins, they are senongue [siblings]." Nonetheless, I am not certain that Holmberg was necessarily in error here since most of my respondents also told me that they didn't marry cousins because it is "against God's will." The Sirionó at present marry according to Western patterns and, like lowland mestizos, consider marriage to first cousins improper. If cross-cousin marriage did exist at one time, the Sirionó either do not remember it or choose not to. In this aspect of Sirionó culture, missionary as well as mestizo influence has been strong and they are acutely aware of conforming to the norms set by the larger society. There is also the possibility that over time, cross-cousin marriage simply became more and more difficult to carry out even without missionary injunction. The rapid depopulation experienced by the Sirionó during the early years of contact, those years in which Holmberg was among them, would have limited available marriage partners. Every family lost many of its members, which would have greatly reduced the numbers of individuals who fell into the category of cross-cousin. Also, during this period of contact and depopulation, dispersed bands of Sirionó were brought together as at Ibiato, opening up new possibilities for potential spouses. As far as I could determine, there was only one cousin marriage in Ibiato and that was between parallel cousins (marrying the offspring of one's mother's sister or father's brother). This marriage was accepted but considered unsuitable.

The women of Ibiato became my best informants since it would have seemed both improper and unnatural for me as a female to spend inordinate amounts of time among the men. As an outsider and a gringa I was permitted more freedom than would normally be allowed, but most of the time I chose to remain within the boundaries established by the Sirionó.

As a female, I was interested in the role of women in the village and their status relative to men. What I ultimately found was basically a continuation of Sirionó band society norms. There was the expected division of labor by sex, but it was also accompanied by the greater egalitarianism found among most foraging peoples of the tropics. In spite of mestizo influence and strongly patriarchal Christian teachings, women have retained a great deal of power and autonomy in their village life. At first I had difficulty in understanding this because the domains of women and men are so different, with men more frequently playing public roles. But as time went on, I began to see the importance of women in both the domestic and public spheres.

For several weeks at least, I had the mistaken impression that women had little involvement in matters that concerned the village as a whole. All I had seen was the two ererecuas meet with the men. And while I was not expressly asked not to attend these meetings, I felt uncomfortable about doing so. The women told me that nothing of real interest ever went on anyway in the men's meetings; and when something important needed discussing, the women would participate as well. At times, the men grumbled at being called to these meetings since they were usually going to be asked to work. I also noticed that now and then some of them, including Chiro, would conveniently plan a hunting trip if they knew in advance that a work day was in the offing.

General meetings, normally taking place inside the church, were called when a crisis arose or a matter affecting the entire community needed attention. One Sunday morning, a theft of money was reported to the ererecuas who then met with the townspeople following church services. This was my first experience with a meeting of this type; and I was curious to see that the women, particularly the younger ones, took an outspoken, aggressive role in voicing their opinions. The thief was never identified, but the public reaction to the robbery made it clear that no one was going to condone this type of behavior. Later on, another general meeting was held to discuss the opening of the school year. It was decided to build a house for the new mestizo teacher, a task the men would complete (but didn't), and to carry out a general cleaning of the school and the grounds around it, something the women would do (and did). This latter chore was entrusted to the Club de Madres (Mother's Club) which, I began to discern, was a source of significant political power in the village. The club had its own meeting place, an empty house that held the communal oven. The men, on the other hand, met out in the open or, in case of inclement weather, in the school or church. The Mothers' Club was also solely responsible for obtaining the food products in Trinidad from CARITAS, arranging for their transport, and overseeing the distribution once they reached Ibiato. When word was sent by radio that "los productos" were on their way to Casarabe by truck or tractor, I was amazed that first time to see the women, totally unassisted, tracking down and catching the horses and riding oxen they would need, saddling them, and then riding off in a group to meet the tractor when it arrived. In a mestizo community, the men would have been expected to take care of this.

The president of the club, Rosa Chiriqui, another of the women who was attending the public health courses in Trinidad, was instrumental in encouraging the club as a whole to start a latrine-building campaign in Ibiato. As a Peace Corps volunteer I had seen such projects met with only mixed enthusiasm, the result being that few people, mostly the organizers, would go along with it while the majority ignored the project. The Mothers' Club, however, carried enough clout to achieve 100 percent compliance. *Every* house now had a latrine, and most were built by the men who had been prodded, bullied, and, if necessary, shamed into completing the work.

On another occasion, one of the mestizo men, Miguel Barbosa, who had been living in his wife's mother's house, set out to build one of his own. He had asked the ererecuas for assistance in getting some of the men to help him carry the larger timbers to the building site. The response had been lukewarm, probably not so much because Miguel was an outsider but because he had few debts to call in. Finally in exasperation, Miguel asked that a general assembly be convened. Miguel stood up at this meeting and gave a short speech about how no one would help him so he was going to take his wife and two small children to Trinidad. The men were silent. First Juana, then Rosa, and finally several other women stood up and let loose a stream of anger at the men's lack of responsibility and charity toward someone who lived in their community. One woman made the comment that people in Casarabe behaved like this, not those of Ibiato. The result was a promise to Miguel that he would have the help he needed. The next morning the men turned out in force to cut and haul posts and thatch.

I also came to realize that it was the women who maintained an interest in the old customs and stories of Sirionó past, truly treasuring the elderly Sirionó as the keepers of tradition. The men were not generally reluctant to delve into the old ways but rather seemed to find them uninteresting. What was past was then, what is now is now. The women, however, loved to talk about the old beliefs, particularly the tales of precontact times. Nancy, Lila, and Mireya made certain that I met the older Sirionó, especially the women, to share in these stories. One of these was Ignacia Cuasu, at least as old as Jêjê and perhaps older. Some told me they thought she was the oldest living Sirionó.

One afternoon, Nancy and her friends took me down to the house near the road where Ignacia was staying with Pastor Mateo Pópole and his family. Ignacia is one of the few Sirionó in Ibiato who never learned to speak Spanish, although she comprehends it to some degree. When we arrived, Ignacia was in her hammock, toes intertwined in the strings. Her hair was cut very short, in the old style, although she no longer plucked the brow hairs. She was addressed by the women not as Ignacia but as *Ari*, Sirionó for grandmother. This word is reserved for only the very old women and is a term of respect and endearment. Mireya immediately took the responsibility of translator, moving smoothly between Spanish and Sirionó.

"Ari," Mireya said, "Tell us again about when the Yanaigua [Ayoreo] captured you." "Yes!" Nancy and Lila said, "Tell us how that came to pass!" Ignacia sat up in her hammock, reaching down to select a ripe mango from the small pile we had placed at her feet. After she had peeled it and sucked off some juice with her gums, she began her story.

"We were out gathering *palmito* [palm heart] one day. We were two women and a man. I had my young son with me. He was small, still at my breast. The Yanaigua were there in the forest. We didn't know they were around and so were talking and laughing while we gathered palmito. They must have heard us, because they were suddenly there, all around us. We were very frightened. I thought they would kill us, but they made us start walking to the south. We walked many days until we came to their camp where there were many, many Yanaiguas. Women and children too. We were made the women's slaves. The women made me nurse their babies as well as my own. My son wasn't getting enough milk and cried a lot. So they killed him because they said he made too much noise. I had to work day and night. I almost never slept. They beat me and only gave me scraps to eat. I didn't think I would live very long. The other two who were with me had already died."

Ignacia's eyes had misted over and had a faraway look. The rest of us were responding with sighs of sympathy. The old woman sucked again from her mango and continued.

"When I thought that I didn't have many more days left, the whites attacked. It was a comisión [she used the Spanish term] that had come to take revenge on the Yanaigua. They had been raiding farms and killing people. They had also stolen some children. The comisión began firing their guns. There was a lot of screaming and people were running around. I took my chance and ran off into the woods. No one noticed me. I began walking north, toward the place where I had been taken. I found things to eat and hid myself well at night. I was lucky, the jaguar didn't catch my scent. After many days, I made my way back to my own people. I had four more sons, but they, too, died. I have no sons and no husband to take care of me now that I am old."

Ignacia looked at us and for a while we said nothing. Then she smiled, and the silence was broken. She seemed content that for a few minutes at least, we had shared the tragedy of her past. Nancy asked her if she needed anything and Ignacia responded that she was fine, Pastor was looking out for her.

As we left the house, Nancy and Mireya suggested we visit a new arrival whom they referred to only as "La Gorda"—neither knew the woman's name. Her house was just down the road beyond Pastor's. "La Gorda" I was told was an enormously fat woman who had arrived a few weeks earlier with her husband. When we came to the house, the woman was sitting on a mat outside. With her legs folded in front of her, she looked like an obese Buddha. I could see why the women had been curious about her; she was certainly an anomaly. She got up from the mat with great difficulty, and I wondered how she had made the trip from wherever she had come.

We all introduced ourselves. The woman's name was Mauricia Jurasayegua. She said that she had come from Salvatierra. I was surprised at this, since I certainly would have remembered her. She then explained that she had been living in her chaco at the time but knew of my presence in the village. Since I had not included her in my Ibiato census, I asked her a few questions, including her age. She said "about 26." I had judged her to be in her late thirties but decided that her weight must have made her seem older. Mauricia told me her father was a Guarayo. (The surname hadn't sounded Sirionó. The Sirionó of Ibiato have taken the names of their fathers as surnames. Those brought up on local ranches took "slave names," the surnames of the people they worked for. Her mother, a Sirionó, was distantly related to Pastor Mateo.) Her husband was Juan Chubirú, a Sirionó who had left Ibiato as a young man to go to Urubichá, eventually ending up in Salvatierra where he met Mauricia. They had not done well economically in Salvatierra so Juan had decided to return to Ibiato, bringing Mauricia with him.

She went on to say that they had no children. She had suffered several miscarriages and once again she was pregnant. About eight months, she thought. Mireya, Nancy, and Lila looked at each other, obviously surprised that this had escaped their scrutiny, but later commenting that with women who are *"muy gorda"* it is hard to tell. Then Mauricia matter-of-factly told us that she would not bear this child as well. A bruja in Salvatierra had told her she would come to Ibiato to die in childbirth.

We visited a while with Mauricia and then walked back to Ibiato. Since she didn't come to the village, Mauricia wasn't a frequent topic of conversation. Most of the new arrivals chose to live as she did, far from the center of community activity. Mauricia and the others not brought up in Ibiato had been raised as nominal Catholics and no doubt were perplexed by the fundamentalist fervor of the community's residents. I wondered if she as well as those people who had experienced only popular religiosity felt uncomfortable in the town proper and so chose to remain on the periphery of village life.

A few weeks after our visit to the houses on the road, we learned that Mauricia had died. The story of her death troubled people, both the suddenness and the manner, as well as the fact that she herself had predicted it.

We had had a period of almost continual rains when Mauricia died. During a particularly bad storm in the middle of the night, Mauricia had gone into labor. Juan, concerned about his wife's condition, went out into the storm to find Pastor Mateo, who accompanied him back to the house. Mauricia was not doing well. Pastor Mateo attempted to determine the position of the fetus, but Mauricia would not hold still. He believed the child was lying in a transverse position and would have to be turned. Mauricia by now was down on the floor, apparently having convulsions. Juan and Pastor tried to control her, but her great size was too much for them. Her struggle did not last long. Her eyes rolled back into her head and she died.

The two men left Mauricia where she lay, trying to decide what to do now that she was dead. The rain continued. In this weather there would be little hope of finding the men necessary to carry her to the cemetery—almost three kilometers away. There was also no way to make a coffin, for it would take a great deal of wood to contain her. Mauricia would have to be buried right there and in a blanket. Three separate graves were started but had to be abandoned because they quickly filled with water seeping in from the low, sodden ground. In desperation, Pastor and Juan chose another site: the side of the road where the terreplein had been built. She was buried in the open on the road to Casarabe.

Not only had Mauricia died a terrible death, I was told, but she had been buried without ritual in an unsuitable place. Not surprisingly, there were soon stories that Mauricia was haunting the road. On his way back from his chaco one night, Cristóbal Eatandu claimed Mauricia walked with him as far as the cemetery and then disappeared. Even Don Adolfo said he saw a large shape, a bulto, beside the road early one day as he traveled from Casarabe to Ibiato. He began to leave Casarabe later in the morning, making certain that it was daylight when he rode by Mauricia's grave.

Nancy and some of the other women were curious about seeing where Mauricia was buried but were afraid to go alone. Then they had an opportunity to make the trip in a large group. I had asked one of the elderly women to show me how the kiakwas were made, the clay pipes used by men and women to smoke tobacco. Both Anderson and Priest have discouraged the use of tobacco, but the older people continue to grow a few stalks and smoke it in their clay pipes. The only clay deposit nearby was along the road to Casarabe, past the place where Mauricia lay. About fifteen women wanted to accompany us, deciding that they would like to gather clay to make some pottery ware for their own use.

We arrived at Mauricia's burial place at noon. The sun was very hot so we took refuge in her recently abandoned house nearby. We could see the three partially dug graves, dry now and beginning to fill with leaves. On the side of the road in front of the house was a large mound, Mauricia's grave. In the bright sunlight the women were not afraid. They gathered around the mound to discuss the tragic event. "Poor Mauricia, you came here only to die." "Oh, Mauricia, not even a coffin to rest in." "Poor Mauricia, look how the cattle have walked all over your grave." Cristóbal Eatandu, who had been visiting Pastor Mateo and saw our group pass by, joined us. He told about how Mauricia's ghost had walked with him. She had asked if he had any bread. There was never any bread in Ibiato, she had said. It was clear that Mauricia's soul was not happy. The women seemed to want to do something to alter the situation, but didn't know what.

I suggested we mark her grave. In Salvatierra, I explained, there were crosses on all the graves and perhaps Mauricia would like this. Everyone agreed it would be a good thing to do. The women went into the forest and selected a hardwood sapling that Cristóbal cut with his machete. He cut a longer and shorter piece, notching them in the middle and tying them together with a piece of vine we had found. Then there was a brief discussion about where the head of the grave lay. Cristóbal volunteered that he thought it was at the western end of the mound. We planted the cross. All of the women gathered once more around the grave, speaking informally to Mauricia and telling her to rest now, there was no need to wander around anymore. Word of our visit rapidly spread through the village, and soon the stories of hauntings ceased.

As an anthropologist, I viewed the episode in a social rather than supernatural context. Mauricia's death had not been dealt with properly and people knew this. They expressed their sense of guilt in terms of Mauricia herself—she was displeased and unhappy and therefore her soul would not rest. Once a death ritual had been performed, no matter how contrived, the community healed its own wounds. Life could now return to normal.

Death is something very familiar to the Sirionó; but in spite of their more than fair share of having to deal with it, they have not grown hardened. In the old days the dying would be abandoned simply because the survival of the group took precedence over feelings for the individual, but there is no evidence that it was done callously. It was a reality of life but still a painful one. Now that the Sirionó are settled, they are not spared the actual moment of death, and it is difficult for them to stand by and watch the passing of a close relative or friend.

For weeks we thought Lucio Irua would certainly die. He had been in the hospital in Trinidad for well over two months; but the doctors had discharged him, telling his family there was nothing more they could do. He was put on a truck and brought back to Ibiato. People said that Lucio had drunk himself into the grave. His years of consuming huge amounts of alcohol had finally caught up with him. His body was swollen from edema and his skin had a yellow cast. For several weeks, Lucio did nothing but lie on cow hide on the floor of his house, refusing to stay in his hammock as was the old custom, and eating and drinking almost nothing. The Sirionó took turns visiting his house to stand a death watch. Except for some of the younger men who espouse the philosophy of *machismo* of mestizo society that men do not cry, everyone who visited Lucio wept openly at his plight. One afternoon when it appeared that he was about to die, his thirteen-year-old son lay down beside him and sobbed, begging his father not to leave him. Most of the villagers had gathered outside the house, joining in the boy's grief.

In spite of the incredible odds against it, Lucio began to recover slowly. The swelling in his limbs subsided and his skin took on a healthier color. Prayers for him were offered at every church service, and in the Cuellar house Chiro and Nancy remembered him at meals when we said grace. People continued to visit Lucio, bringing him small gifts of food and drink, often preparing special items that might encourage him to eat. Before I left Ibiato, Lucio was back in his hammock, certainly not robust but at least looking as though he would survive.

CHAPTER ELEVEN

At these times of great crisis, the small hatreds and disputes that seemed to go on without respite were tempered by a need for the community to pull together. Then the true solidarity of the village was evident, and, for a while at least, animosities would be put aside in favor of the greater good. When the crisis had passed, the community would settle back into old routines of day-to-day existence: gathering firewood, cooking meals, going to church, bringing in produce from the chacos, hunting, and, of course, to lend spice to it all, gossiping about family and neighbors.

When the time arrived for me to leave Ibiato, I felt I had come to understand something about the rhythm of life there, to know something about the ways of the Sirionó, and to worry about their uncertain future. Many I came to know more than just casually, becoming involved in their lives as they did in mine. I was an outsider and an observer, two roles that always influenced my place in the community. But I was also accepted and welcomed, and while the people may not have always understood the reasons for my many questions, they were always willing to try to explain their way of life to me. In this regard, it was consistent that Nancy would suggest that I should not leave before seeing the older men perform the Hito-Hito, the circle dance and chant. We spoke to Daniel about it, and he agreed to call the men together the following Sunday, my last full day in Ibiato.

The afternooon of the dance was clear and warm. We had had several days of hot weather so the plaza was dry. Daniel and Arturo rang the church bell, but already people had begun to gather, word of the impending event having spread. When a good crowd had formed and the men were laughing and comfortable with themselves and the rest of us, Daniel, Arturo, and Edilberto locked arms behind their backs, threw their heads back, and began stamping their feet in rhythm. Soon the other senior men joined them, locking arms to form a larger circle. Daniel, the oldest and most respected male, chanted the Hito-Hito, an old dance performed in precontact times to celebrate a good hunt or a general feeling that all was well with the world. After a while, even the women and children joined in, some trying to follow the words as Daniel chanted:

> Hito! Hito! Hito! Hito!
> A cha jisare mose!
> A ji sue cha!
> A cha ibachi cha!
> A cha mimba mimba!
> Hito!
> > Hito!
> > > Hito!
> > > > Hito . . .

Happiness! Happiness! Happiness! Happiness!
When there are many little toucans!
When there are little animals in their nests!
When the corn is young!
When there is palm fruit!
Happiness!
      Happiness!
           Happiness!
               Happiness...

"ARTURO"

Part
Three

TWELVE
Chapter 12

$\mathbf{A}$t a recent meeting of anthropologists, I delivered a paper on the current situation of the Sirionó. When I had finished, a colleague asked me the inevitable question: What did I think were the prospects for Sirionó cultural survival at Ibiato? Given that I had only a few moments to respond, I answered somewhat glibly that I thought there was a good chance for a positive future for these people as a society. But the question is a complex one, and I have real misgivings about being overly optimistic. Cultural survival in Ibiato hinges on several factors, most of which are beyond the immediate control of the Sirionó. Should the present, generally positive situation begin to degenerate for any reason, the continuation of the Sirionó as a group would be severely threatened. I have mentioned some of these problems in the course of this narrative. Now, in this final chapter, I would like to explore more fully those factors that I feel may ultimately determine Sirionó success or failure.

LAND

The provision of land for native peoples is probably the single most important issue in their survival, yet it is the most difficult to ensure. Typically, land occupied by hunters and gatherers is considered "vacant" by those who would like to exploit it. Particularly in South America where development has become the imperative of every nation, undeveloped land must be put to "productive" use. This usually means agriculture—farming or ranching. That good land should sit idle, to be used only by a handful of foragers or small-scale horticulturists, is seen as contrary to most developmental objectives. Consequently, it is very difficult for Indian peoples to defend their rights to lands they have occupied for generations.

In this, the Sirionó are fortunate. While 7,000 hectares is not a great deal of land, it provides for their present agricultural needs as well as those of the foreseeable future. The fact that they are not settled in an area widely suitable for horticulture has enabled the Sirionó to concern themselves only infrequently about losing their land to squatters. There is an interesting parallel here with the Panare of Venezuela, who also inhabit a grassland that they have shared successfully with mestizo ranchers for over a hundred years. Like the Sirionó, the Panare are free to hunt the grasslands and nearby forests, experiencing little competition from local mestizos who are provided with meat from their cattle herds.

In the Venezuelan case, the land is arid and therefore suitable only for cattle raising. Nonetheless, the fact that the region is considered "open" land has recently encouraged higher rates of mestizo settlement, stressing the normally peaceful relations between Panare and settler. In the Beni, the greatest threat to Sirionó hunting is the possibility of converting pastureland to plow agriculture. The high humidity of the region could make rice production a potentially successful alternative to cattle ranching. To date, however, the capital investment in equipment and the low market value of rice has precluded any large-scale shift in the traditional economy of the region. Cattle ranching remains highly cost effective: there is little inversion in labor, land, or equipment, and beef prices usually far outstrip those for field crops. Then there is always the problem of transportation. Low overhead and high market value of beef makes it possible to fly out carcasses to Bolivian cities. It would be economically unfeasible to attempt this with rice or corn. If transportation networks in the Beni should improve, however, it is conceivable that frontier expansion such as that occurring in Santa Cruz would begin to impinge on the forests of the Beni as well. While ranchers would probably continue to be involved primarily in the production of beef, new transport routes would attract small farmers into the region at an unprecedented rate. Large holdings with forest reserves, such as those of the Sirionó, would come under immediate pressure for settlement.

At present, the major problem facing the Sirionó is obtaining a clear title to their land. The titling process in Bolivia is a long and arduous one, taking constant legal attention with its attendant costs. It is unlikely that the Sirionó themselves will be able to carry their case forward. Therefore, they, like so many native groups, are dependent on advocacy from other sources. If APCOB is successful in gaining title for Sirionó lands, the Sirionó will be in a much stronger position. It should also be noted that not all the Sirionó at Ibiato are in favor of designating the land an Indigenous Community (Comunidad Indígena). Just as the communal herd is a source of friction, to a lesser degree so is communal land. Some Sirionó would prefer to have separate title to their holdings, giving them the option of selling. However it might contribute to individual incentive, this approach would rapidly bring about the destruction of Ibiato as a community. It would not take the local mestizos long to figure out ways to divest individual Sirionó of their land.

Assuming the Sirionó are able to obtain a title to the lands of Ibiato, they will still be faced with the potential problem of squatters and non-Sirionó inhabitants. Bolivia recognizes squatters' rights once actual residence has been established. Thus, the Sirionó will have to maintain constant vigilance against invasions of their land. So far, they have been successful in doing this; but they also have had the benefit of advance warning and the encouragement and support of Anderson. Then too, the attempts at squatting have been localized and consisted of relatively few settlers—squatting has only presented minor headaches now and then. Should it become more frequent and widespread, the Sirionó will have a much more difficult time dealing with the problem. Theoretically, they could be kept so busy trying to protect their boundaries in addition to their other subsistence pursuits that some areas could go unprotected. At that point, it would be relatively simple for squatters to establish a permanent settlement. Once this foothold had been secured, it would only be a matter of time before they spread over the land virtually unchecked.

Last, the Sirionó could lose control of their land by allowing greater numbers of non-Sirionó to take up residence there through marriage. Thus far this pattern has been tempered by present policies that prevent outsiders from remaining in Ibiato should the union be dissolved. Although the Sirionó generally agree with this practice, it was instituted by the missionaries. There is, therefore, no guarantee that once missionary influence is withdrawn the Sirionó will continue to enforce this rule. Unfortunately, except for perhaps Chiro and Daniel, the Sirionó do not reflect on the ultimate consequences of losing their land; many have even had to be goaded into confronting squatters. This somewhat cavalier attitude about the land may come as a result of Ibiato's longevity and, therefore, its perceived inalienability. For some Sirionó, at least, it is inconceivable that Ibiato will not always be there. Others take a more fatalistic attitude. When I asked them what they would do if their land were to be taken away, they shrugged their shoulders and answered, "We would just go far out into the wilderness and build a new village." What they failed to comprehend is that there is less and less wilderness that does not have some prior claim.

SUBSISTENCE

Land means not only having a place to exist but also being able to maintain a qualilty of life that is conducive to well-being. At present, the Sirionó have found an equilibrium between farming and hunting, allowing them to meet their subsistence needs as well as having minimal access to a cash economy. In terms of farming, the current landholdings worked by the Sirionó are more than adequate. The rotational requirements of slash-and-burn horticulture are being met with neither labor nor land being stressed beyond reasonable carrying capacities. And while Sirionó land itself does not meet their needs for successful hunting, they have not been restricted from going farther afield.

The importance of hunting to basic Sirionó well-being cannot be over-emphasized. Hunting contributes most of their protein, lessening their dependence on outside sources or on less dependable and poorer substitutes of vegetable protein. The Sirionó at Ibiato are in relatively good health, in stark contrast to those at Salvatierra and elsewhere where food and meat supplies are much scarcer. Hunting also provides a stable source of income. Although the returns may be small, the selling of skins brings in enough income to purchase such necessities as medicines, kerosene, shotgun shells, salt, and other commodities. It should also be mentioned that hunting as a source of income is consistent with Sirionó patterns for achieving power and prestige. Rather than create a competitive situation where power is gained solely by economic superiority, hunting provides cash income without upsetting traditional values. Earning substantial income from hunting requires skill as well as luck, and the good hunter has always been esteemed. There also exists the understanding that anyone who applies himself steadily to hunting will become better at it and will simply have more opportunities to bring in game. Rather than incur envy and hostility, such perseverance brings respect. Then, too, hunting success is always limited to factors outside the control of the hunter: seasonality, weather, and game densities. Thus it is relatively difficult for any single individual to vastly outperform his peers in terms of economic advantages derived from hunting. Last, the psychological importance of hunting must be considered. To the Sirionó, hunting brings all those things that are worthwhile in life: status, respect, good health, and good times. Even the women look forward to going on an ito, a long hunt that takes them into the wilderness for a week or two. It is a time of renewal, a period away from the stresses of village life.

To date, the continuity of life in Ibiato has been sheltered by the relative lack of development in the region of the Beni where they live. Ranching has been compatible with the Sirionó life-style, creating a symbiosis between rancher and hunter. The lack of competition between the Sirionó and their rancher neighbors has enabled them to pursue a way of life that is rapidly disappearing in other areas of the lowlands where population pressure has been increasing. The perseverance of the Sirionó way of life thus depends on a maintenance of the status quo. Should ranchers sell out to agriculturalists or themselves become farmers, all would change. In a worst case situation, the Sirionó of Ibiato would probably end up dispersed through the region, as many of them are now, working for others as peons.

LEADERSHIP

The training of leaders who can deal effectively with internal as well as external problems is another key factor in the survival of any group. It is in this realm that missionaries most commonly cause havoc by creating new leaders who are not necessarily recognized as such by their own people. The result frequently is to divide the group's loyalty between its traditional leaders and the new, religious leaders, the latter commonly having more power because of their contacts with the outside. Fortunately, this pattern has failed to develop in Ibiato, although not as the result of any missionary insight. Rather, the preservation of traditional leadership and the gradual introduction of modern leaders derives from the subtle rivalry between Anderson and Priest and, more specifically, from Anderson's greater influence in the community.

Jack Anderson is an old-style missionary, but different even from others of his era in that he had little formal training or education. Consequently, his "methodology" for establishing a mission was a seat-of-the-pants effort based on his own experience. Because of his lack of proper missionary indoctrination, he identified very closely with the Sirionó, often accepting their ways of doing things without critical evaluation—an evaluation that could only have come from a prior mind-set. Thus it never really occurred to Jack to try to create new leaders to guide the Sirionó into Christianity—that was his job. He respected the old leaders, many of whom were thankful for his protection and who became his loyal friends and compatriots. Jack gives as much credit to these early ererecuas as he does to himself for the establishment of Ibiato.

Perry Priest with his SIL training came from a different and much more cerebral tradition. He studied a body of mission doctrine that defined very clearly how to accomplish certain cultural changes designed to make people more receptive to Christianity. One of these was to select young men, remove them temporarily from the community, and train them as catequists and potential village leaders. In the Sirionó case, Jack's continued support of the old leaders and the maintenance of hereditary leadership through lines of ererecuas effectively blocked early attempts by some of the young trainees to take over leadership positions. They were accepted as religious leaders, and Jack encouraged this as well; but the governing of the village remained with the ererecuas, perpetuating the continuity of power and authority according to tradition.

In another departure from SIL expectations, it is unlikely that those men who do not come from a "chiefly" line will ever be given an opportunity to become ererecuas. However, the schooling of Sirionó men in Tumi Chuqua covered a broad enough range that there will be no lack of possible candidates. Men like Chiro and Vicente possess many of the traditional qualifications for leadership, including birthright, in addition to their skills acquired at the SIL training camp. As I have shown, the younger, more acculturated men can move easily into brokerage rules when necessary; but they are also careful not to do this in a way that would threaten the status or respect of the ererecuas. By supporting the old system, these potential leaders now have a vested interest in seeing that the ererecua keeps his power and authority—after all, they will be taking over those positions in the near future.

The biggest question that remains concerns the leadership gap left by Perry Priest's departure from Bolivia and by Anderson's advanced age. Both of these men have interceded on Ibiato's behalf on countless occasions, using their positions as missionaries and status as Americans to significant advantage. No matter how well trained in leadership even Chiro may be, he will never have the resources necessary to lobby for his people as effectively as the two missionaries, particularly at the national level. This ultimately may affect the Sirionós' ability to maintain their land rights and their educational advantages. The Sirionó may be living in a house of cards that will collapse once Anderson and Priest are no longer there to shore it up. Only time will determine how effective the native leaders will be in fighting for those causes that will determine success or defeat of the Sirionó as a people.

POPULATION

In addition to land, subsistence, and leadership, we also must consider numbers of people. Anthropologists familiar with native populations know there is a "magic number" of 500 necessary for survival. While not a hard and fast rule, studies have shown that when a group has less than 500 members it is difficult for it to continue as a cultural entity. Ibiato, with only 267 people, falls far short of this limit. What then are the prospects for future population growth? Is the village actually in a decline? According to Anderson, Ibiato at one time numbered over 600 inhabitants, but disease rapidly reduced this number to less than 400. Then there was a period when people left to go elsewhere, continuing a seminomadic existence. Some returned, but most were never heard from again. According to Priest who had visited the community regularly for the past fifteen years or so, the population seems to have stabilized and may even be growing slightly. The number of children being born and their improved chances for survival give hope that Ibiato's inhabitants may be slowly increasing. While in-migration is not occurring on a large scale, it too is contributing to the base population as well as that of the future. The continuing growth of Ibiato will depend on the maintenance of dietary levels, preventive health care, economic and educational opportunities, and a sense of well-being that encourages people to remain there. If present population levels continue to increase, Ibiato could attain 500 residents in a matter of a few years.

There may, however, be other considerations. With 500 or more people, the village's resources may be stressed, particularly game animals. From all appearances, animals are being hunted at a rate that allows for reproduction and replacement. Hence, there has been no significant drop in hunting success during Ibiato's more than fifty years of existence. When the population reached 600, it did so for a very short time, giving no indication whether that number of people could be supported by the surrounding region. Having more people would also alter the relationship with other local inhabitants, creating stresses that may not be in existence at present. This, too, could jeopardize the security of the village. Thus while population growth may be necessary to maintain some predetermined limit for cultural survival, it could also create problems that would threaten that very survival. Perhaps for the Sirionó in their current situation, 300 may be their "magic number."

COMMUNITY SOLIDARITY

Finally, we must discuss something really quite intangible—the ethos of the village. Is there a feeling of community in Ibiato adequate to bind the people together if they are faced with major threats to their continuation as a group? Is their sense of being Sirionó well-developed enough to stand up against pressures on them as individuals? In their precontact state, the sense of membership in a larger group was not particularly strong. They were simply "mbia," "people," whose primary loyalties were to their own local bands consisting of extended kin. There were no annual "tribal" gatherings or ritual assemblies that intensified sentiments of belonging to a unified society. The Sirionó had a long tradition of being pursued by other Indians as well as by mestizos, living a precarious existence of only fleeting stability. For most, being settled at Ibiato was their first understanding that there were so many others like them, so many of their own kind.

Pride in being Sirionó still is not a universal sentiment among the Sirionó of Ibiato. While Jack was among them, he was basically unaware of such issues as ethnic solidarity. He kept the Sirionó separated from the larger society primarily because he recognized its "tainting" influence—he did not want the village corrupted by the outside world. As a consequence, most of the older Sirionó are unconcerned about problems of ethnic identity. They are who they are. There are more important things in their lives, such as

147

getting in a crop and securing enough meat. A few of the younger Sirionó, especially those who have been away from the village for some time, are also unconcerned with their native origins. Ibiato is where their families live, their friends and relatives. It is not necessarily a sacred homeland. Being Sirionó for them is something they are while among their own people. Once in the world at large, they make every effort to be like everyone else. But many others, primarily those who were schooled at Tumi Chuqua, have been instilled with ideas of "native consciousness." The importance of maintaining the Sirionó language has always been stressed by Perry Priest and, along with it, the customs and traditions that make the Sirionó unique. These individuals now make up an outspoken majority in the community, publicly denouncing efforts to denigrate Sirionó heritage.

As a result of SIL influence, Ibiato adopted August 2, the national "Day of the Indian," as its feast day. As a Protestant mission, Ibiato had no Saint's Day to celebrate, something which, as the Sirionó became more aware of it, made them feel out of step with other communities. Thus, every August 2 the town holds a festival, inviting anyone who would like to attend, providing food and entertainment in the form of bow and arrow competitions and traditional dancing.

What has set Ibiato apart as a distinct community, however, is not only its native origins but its status as a Protestant stronghold. This by itself makes the village "special" in the eyes of its residents. They consider themselves to be creyentes, "true believers," as opposed to their neighbors who are "only" Catholics. As a result, they are not only Sirionó but Christians as well, singled out to see that the word of God is not lost. Therefore, the rewards for maintaining boundaries around their community are not just in preserving their purity as a people but in stemming the flow of nonbelievers, heretics, who would threaten the very sanctity of the village. If this philosophy survives the withdrawal of the missionaries, it may act as another bond to preserve Ibiato's integrity as a Sirionó community. The combination of a strong religious as well as ethnic identity could prove invincible in the face of attempts to dismantle their solidarity. That the Sirionó can and are willing to stand up to such threats is exemplified by an incident that occurred during the annual August fiesta. Nancy was standing next to a well-dressed woman from Casarabe who had come to share in the festivities. The woman leaned over toward Nancy and whispered, "I understand all these people are Choris!" Nancy leaned back responding, "Yes, you are right. And I am one of them!"

Figure 7. The People of Ibiato

At the time of Allan Holmberg's research, he estimated that there were 2000 Sirionó. These are the people of Ibiato, the last Sirionó, as counted in 1984. Many of the ages, especially of older people, are estimates.

Name	Age
1. Julio Cangue	47
2. Ana María	47
3. Pascual Ajei	23
4. Irma Ẽtea	16
5. Selinda Ajei	5
6. María Equatãya	50
7. Ismael Ajei	8
8. Edilberto Yoseté	45
9. Marta Moreno	36
10. René Antelo	12
11. Guido Sánchez	35
12. Marina Eato	25
13. Dario Sánchez	18
14. Milda Sánchez	15
15. Chelo Sánchez	10
16. Alicia Sánchez	2
17. Hernán Eato	42
18. Rosa Mano	32
19. Ana Eato	16
20. Rufino Eato	12
21. Rogel Eato	7
22. Silvia Eato	4
23. Milisia Eato	2½
*24. Serafin Varga	30
25. Betty Chiri	35
26. Babi Guirayka	16
27. Quitín Guirayka	8½
28. Lupe Guirayka	6
29. Elyda Churuka	6
30. Chalfa Churuka	24
31. Juan Chubirú	34
32. Mauricia Jurasayequa	29(d.4/4/84)
33. Germán Pópole	53
34. Marcia Señorita	50

Name	Age
35. Julia Chiriqui	45
36. Humberto Monje	50
37. Félix Monje	12
38. Nego Monje	4
39. Florida Campo	50
40. Pastor Mateo Pópole	55
41. Ignacia Cuasu	70
42. Victor Chiri	60
43. Yesi	50
44. Juan Eatosa	21
45. Rafael Eatosa	15
46. Rosana Eatosa	9
47. Victor Chiri (son)	2
*48. Edgar Daza	22
49. Teresa Mateo	25
50. Juan Carlos	4
51. Cleotilde Daza	3
52. Edgar Daza	9 mos.
53. Pedro Yaves	58
54. Rosa Chiriqui	40
55. Juliana Yaves	13
56. Casilda Yaves	13
57. Gabriel Yaves	4
58. Pedro Yaves (son)	2
59. Juan Eatandu	50
60. Darlene Ticuasu	25
61. China Eatandu	4
62. Yoni Eatandu	10 mos.
63. Bob Eatandu	48
64. Hilda Chiriqui	45
65. Victor Eatandu	18
66. Raquel Eatandu	9
67. Ovidio Ticuasu	50
68. Telma Eritaruki	55
69. Robinson Ticuasu	17
70. Marvin Ticuasu	6
71. Demetrio Guirakangue López	42
72. Elena Ribera	50
73. Emilio López	6
74. Marilu Parique	18

Name	Age
75. Erving Niko	18
76. Carina Niko	9 mos.
77. Bernarda Melgar	15
*78. Aiquile Céspedes Solano	40
79. Juana Eirubi	32
80. Damián Sosa	14
81. Pablo Sosa	11
82. Erving Sosa	9
83. Juan Pablo Sosa	3
84. Manuel Céspedes	6
85. Odalí Céspedes	1 mo.
86. Chiro Cuellar	35
87. Nancy Melgar	28
88. William Cuellar	17
89. Catalina Cuellar	10
90. Wilfredo (Pepe) Cuellar	9
91. Magdalena Cuellar	8
92. Mábel Cuellar	6
93. Emmy Cuellar	4
94. Priscila Cuellar	1½
*95. Miguel Barbosa	61
96. Leti Nova	20
97. Dori Barbosa	2½
98. Angel Barbosa	5 mos.
99. Julio Novachico	40
100. Zoila Quicuandu	40
101. Nataniel Jacinto	24
102. Dalia Sosa Eirubi	16
103. Claribel Jacinto	2
104. Nataniel Jacinto (son)	1
105. Vicente Ino	65
106. Isabel Nanguitendu	46
107. Barbina Ino	1
108. Irma Ino	7
109. Pancho Melgar	50
110. Mañuela Yacu	55
111. Carlos Eirubi	60
112. Susana Yicarere	45
113. Doroty Eirubi	25
114. Wilson Melgar	25

Name	Age
115. Ruth Melgar	12
116. Lorgio Melgar	10
117. Wilsito Melgar	5
118. Eduardo Melgar	4
119. Marilene Melgar	2 mos.
120. Julio Bei	60
121. Dorotea Siririmo	55
122. Jaime Nacae	15
123. Kende Bei	10
124. Daniel Mayacharé	52
125. Modesta Ererededneña	50
126. Benjamín Mayacharé	15
127. Mery Mayacharé	33
128. Mario Eanta	30
129. Aramyo Eanta	8
130. Emilia Eanta	4
131. Ribana Eanta	2
132. Agustín Eatandu	29
133. Petrona Yicarere	22
134. Hugo Yicarere	19
135. Bera Nacae	17
136. Amaua Yicarere	15
136. Alfonso Yicarere	11
138. Fernando Yicarere	9
139. Angela Yicarere	13
140. Tomasa Carranza	60
141. Luisa Carranza	35
142. Roberto López	40
143. Edita López	15
144. Martita López	9
145. Roberto López (son)	6
146. Pablo López	4
147. Mariano López	2
148. Epifanio Campo	50
149. Ernestina Ecabosendu	50
150. Zoilo Mikae	25
151. Mireya Súarez	23
152. Arminda Mikae	7
153. Graciela Mikae	4
154. Ezekiel Mikae	3

Name	Age
155. Clemente Súarez	60
156. Pedro (Chuchú) Pepe	36
157. Mari Irua	27
158. Mirian Pepe	10
159. Alejandrina Pepe	8
160. Pura Pepe	5
161. (Infant) Pepe	4 mos.
162. Blanca Echevey	50
163. Lucio Irua	47
164. Orlando Irua	12
165. Ignacia Méndez	46
166. Edgar Quirindendu	19
167. Olinda Richards	19
168. Rosa Quirindendu	7
169. Esteban Quirindendu	18
179. Susana Moreno	23
171. Segundo Quirindendu	17
172. Selina Quirindendu	16
173. Cristina Quirindendu	13
174. Echavela Quirindendu	10
175. Samuel Quirindenu	5
176. Juan Balcazar Gamarra	38
177. Caludio Eanta	50
178. Victoria Naguandu	50
179. Lunchi Eanta	20
180. Marta Richards	22
181. Yamila Eanta	6
182. Froilán Eanta	3½
183. Erlán Eanta	1
184. Hernán Eanta	1
185. Miguelina Babandu Ciervo	14
186. Echope	50
187. Simona Richards	55
188. Marcia Eanta	14
189. Benjamín (Choco) Guarua	30
190. Lila Suárez	20
191. Alcides Guarua	10
192. Davico Guarua	6
193. Francisco Guarua	3
194. Yolanda Guarua	1

Name	Age
195. Rolli Guarua	17
196. Isora Suárez	19
*197. Angel (Kollita) Umaday	23
198. Carmelo Cahuana	36
199. Justina Erachendu	32
200. Ester Cahuana	15
201. Angel Cahuana	10
202. Rogelia Cahuana	8
203. Clotilde Cahuana	6
204. Bella Cahuana	5
205. Carmelo Cahuana (son)	9 mos.
206. Eloy Erachendu	60
207. Josefa Echivoy	60
208. Nestor Moreno	52
209. Cornelio Ino	19
210. Román Ino	15
211. Eddy Ino	45
212. Asunta Babandu	50
213. Cristina Richards	55
214. Jorge Niko	12
215. Jaime Echivó	52
216. Ramón Babandu Ciervo	48
217. Arturo Eanta	52
218. María	50
219. Ersilla Eanta	20
220. Santo Ribero	20
221. Raúl Eanta	25
222. Nelsi Irua	28
223. Eva Eanta	3
224. Cristián Eanta	11 mos.
225. Elizabet Ribero	2
226. Olga	50
227. Cristóbal Eatandu	48
228. Armando Eatandu	18
229. Saida Quiragangue	16
230. Armadito Eatandu	6 mos.
231. Hortensia Eata	3
232. Erisón Añez	30
233. Berta Baroto	23
234. Chila Añez	6

Name	Age
235. Guillermo Baroto	21
236. Joaquin Yarasi	63
237. Lucho Cuellar	47
238. Martina Mañatingaré	55
239. Juan Té	42
240. Luís Yocoí	62
241. Petrona	50
242. Simon Cuellar	60
243. María Arias	60
244. Jesús Tachi	45
245. Tomasa Rivera	60
246. Alberto Ribera	20
247. Dora Arias	60
248. Abrahán Ribera	5
249. Verónica Ribera	10 mos.
250. Sergio Sembiri	45
251. Rosa	60
252. Bautista Tiquise	52
253. María	60
254. Haroldo Yicarere	40
255. Celia Eremondu	39
256. Poly Yicarere	6
257. Alfredo Yicarere	3
258. Benancio Suárez	50
259. Elsa Ticuasu	33
260. Jelson Suárez	17
261. Lisandro Suárez	16
262. Jorge Suárez	12
263. Freddy Suárez	5
264. Andrés Suárez	1
265. Antonio Quicuandu	60
266. Margarita	60
267. Agusto Mercado	25

*Not Sirionó

Glossary

All words listed are Spanish unless otherwise indicated.

aguaí
(Sideroxylon spp.)

A large, round fruit with a yellow skin and white pulpy interior; may be eaten raw, roasted, or boiled

alcalde

Mayor of a town

anta
(Tapirus terrestris)

Tapir

ari

(Sirionó) Grandmother, old woman

arroba

A dry measure of 25 pounds

arroyo

A creek or small stream

asahi
(Cocos botriofera)

A tall, slim palm tree

bárbaro

Uncivilized person; savage

barraca

A small homestead built on the bank of a river

biscocho

A hard biscuit made from cornmeal, usually round like a small donut

brujo/bruja

Sorcerer or sorceress, someone who uses magic for evil purposes

bulto

A shade or formless shape; in eastern Bolivia the spirits of the dead are said to wander in this way

cacique

A village headman; the term is normally applied only to indigenous leaders

camba

Term used in Bolivia by lowlanders and highlanders to designate a person from the *Oriente*, or lowlands

carpido

Weeded; this is done with a scuffling hoe, or *pala*, which is run over the surface of the ground, cutting off the weeds at ground level

caiman
(Caiman)

South American alligator

157

casero	Someone charged with caring for a house or property in the absence of the owner
cepe *(Atta sp.)*	A leaf-cutter ant
chaco	Cultivated land, in particular land worked by slash-and-burn horticultural methods
chicha	A beer made from corn, manioc, or sweet potatoes; its alcoholic content varies according to length of fermentation
chonta *(Bactrus sp.)*	A palm used for its hard, fibrous wood as well as clusters of fruit
chori	A lowland term of uncertain origin designating forest nomads; also used synonymously with *bárbaro* to mean savage.
chuchillo *(Ginerium sagitatum)*	A type of reed that grows along the edge of rivers; its flower stem is used to make arrow shafts
comisión	A "comission," the term used to designate a group of men formed for a particular task; the word was applied to groups of men sent out to hunt Indians
comité cívica	"Civic Committee," a group in Trinidad formed to exert political pressure on the national government of Bolivia
comunidad indígena	Indigenous community, a legal designation that provides for communal land holdings
contrabandista	A person engaged in some type of illegal trading activity
corregidor	A town magistrate
creyente	A "believer;" the term is applied to Protestant Christians
cumplido	Responsible, trustworthy
cuota	A quota, typically a way of collecting money for a particular communal need; each individual or family is assessed a head tax
curandero	A healer, usually someone knowledgeable in the use of herbal remedies, or having some special healing power or skill
empanizado	Hard, brown sugar made into a flat cake
entendido	Rational, logical, knowledgeable

ererecua	(Sirionó) The leader of a Sirionó band; now, a village headman or *cacique*, a hereditary office
fiesta patronal	Patron's feast; the days set aside each year to celebrate the patron saint of a community
forestal	A forestry agent
hechicería	Witchcraft, spell-casting
huasca	A braided, raw-hide whip used to punish people. The origin of the word is from Quechua, *waska*, a braided rope.
intendente	A military officer or government official placed in a village to maintain order, similar to a police chief or sheriff
item	A line item in a fiscal budget
ito	(Sirionó) (also ITO-ITO) a long hunt, a hunting trip that takes several days
kiakwa	(Sirionó) A clay pipe used for smoking native tobacco
kimbai	(Sirionó) Man, male
kolla	A term derived from the Quechua word Kollasuyo, or that part of the Inca empire pertaining to modern Bolivia; nowadays it designates a person of highland origin as opposed to Camba, or lowlander
macho	Male, masculine, manly, the characteristics associated with qualities of manhood
maestro rural	Rural teacher; a special designation for those teachers trained to work in small, isolated villages
masaco	A lowland staple dish of plantains roasted or boiled and then mashed in a tacú, mortar, with hot fat and salt
mayordomo	A man placed in charge of managing a cattle operation

mestizo	Mixed; a person of European, Indian, and perhaps African cultural and racial heritage; they also may be termed "white" (*blanco*) if they have achieved a place of social and economic importance
motacú (*Attalea princeps*)	A large palm tree whose fronds are used for roofing; also has an edible fruit by the same name
movimiento	Movement, activity; applied to describe whether a town has social activity, places to go, night life, etc.
oriente	The east; eastern or lowland regions of Bolivia
paba	(Sirionó) Father; the father of the band; its leader or ererecua
paja cedrón (*Cymbopogon citratus*)	Lemon grass, made into an aromatic tea that is reputed to have medicinal qualities
palmito	Palm heart, taken from the center of the palm crown; can be eaten raw or cooked
panacú	(Guaraní) A woven palm backpack used to carry meat, firewood, or other products; the Sirionó have adopted this word (their term was *Jiracô*)
paripari	(Sirionó) crazy, unbalanced
partero	A male midwife; relatively rare
pascana	A campsite; an overnight stopping place on a journey
patrón	Landowner; person who keeps indentured laborers tied to the land; a feudal landlord
patujú (*Heliconia bihai*)	A broad-leafed plant that grows in low, wet areas
pensión	A place where meals are taken; a family-style hotel
pícaro	Rogue, thief, untrustworthy person, shyster
plátano (*Musa paradisiaca.*)	Plantain

ración	Ration; staple supplies given to ranch hands each month as part of their work benefits
reducción	A mission established originally by the Jesuits or Franciscans at which nomadic Indians were "reduced" or obliged to remain settled
repasar	The custom of spouse-swapping practiced by the Sirionó
rescatador	A speculator in agricultural products, particularly rice
rozar	The process of cutting low brush in the preparation of a field for burning and planting
senongüe	(Sirionó) Sibling; literally, *my* sibling (*enongue*, his sibling)
surazo	A souther, the cold wind and rain that move through South America from the Antarctic
tacú	A hollowed-out log used as a mortar to grind grain or mash food
taitetú *(Tayassu tajacu)*	Collared peccary
tarea	A measure of land 10×100 meters; the term derives from the word "task" and originally meant the amount of land that could be cultivated in one day
tigre *(Felis onca)*	Tiger, the word used by most lowlanders when referring to the jaguar
trapiche	A large, wooden sugarcane press consisting of several carved gears through which the cane passes and is pressed; commonly turned by horses or oxen
tumbar	To fell; the process of felling large trees in a field once the brush has been cut or *rozado*
turuquia	(Sirionó) Literally, sky; places where forest breaks into savanna and the sky can be seen; bare pampa
tuyua	(Sirionó) The crude shelter built by the Sirionó during precontact times, consisting of palm fronds stacked up against poles

GLOSSARY

uru e   (Sirionó) Someone who doesn't comprehend or ignores the rules

vaquero   Cowboy

yande   (Sirionó) Potential spouse, fiancé(e) sweetheart

yomomal, yomomo   Large areas of floating grass; grass lakes

yuca *(Manihot esculenta)*   Sweet manioc

References

Cardús, José
  1886   *Las Misiones Franciscanas Entre los Infieles de Bolivia.*
          Barcelona: Librería de la Inmaculada Concepción.
Coimbra Sanz, Germán
  1980   *Mitologia Sirionó.* Departmento de Publicaciones. Santa
          Cruz, Bolivia: Universidad Gabriel René Moreno.
Denevan, William
  1963   "Cattle Ranching in the Mojos Savannas of Northeastern
          Bolivia." *Yearbook of the Association of Pacific Coast
          Geographers* 25:37–44.
  1966   "The Aboriginal Cultural Geography of the Llanos de
          Mojos of Bolivia." *Ibero-Americana* 48. Berkeley and Los
          Angeles: University of California Press.
Eyde, David B., and Paul M. Postal
  1963   "Matrilineality and Matrilocality Among the Sirionó: A
          Reply to Needham." *Bijdragen Tot de Taal-, Land-, en
          Volkerkunde.* 119:184–285.
Gross, Daniel R.
  1983   "Village Movement in Relation to Resources in
          Amazonia. In *Adaptive Responses of Native Amazonians,*
          by Raymond B. Hames and William T. Vickers. New
          York: Academic Press.
Hames, Raymond B., and William T. Vickers
  1983   *Adaptive Responses for Native Amazonians.* New York:
          Academic Press.
Holmberg, Allan
  1946   "The Sirionó. A Study of the Effect of Hunger Frustration
          on the Culture of a Semi-Nomadic Bolivian Indian Soci-
          ety." Ph.D. dissertation, Yale University.
  1950   *Nomads of the Long Bow: The Sirionó of Eastern
          Bolivia.* Institute of Social Anthropology, publication no.
          10. Washington: Smithsonian Institution.
  1969   *Nomads of the Long Bow.* Garden City, NY: American
          Museum of Natural History Press.
Howard, Jane
  1984   *Margaret Mead: A Life.* New York: Simon and Schuster.
          (Quotation from Theodore Schwartz, p. 303).
Hvalkof, Soren, and Peter Aaby, eds.
  1981   *Is God an American? An Anthropological Perspective on*

REFERENCES

*the Missionary Work of the Summer Institute of
Linguistics.* International Work Group for Indigenous
Affairs (IWGIA) and Survival International. Denmark:
Vinderup Bogtrykkeri.

Isaac, Barry
    1977   "The Sirionó of Eastern Bolivia: A Reexamination."
            Human Ecology 5:137–54.

Jones, James
    1980   "Conflict Between Whites and Indians on the Llanos de
            Moxos, Beni Department: A Case Study in Development
            from the Cattle Regions of the Bolivian Oriente." Ph.D.
            dissertation, University of Florida.

Kelm, Heinz
    1967   "O Canto Matinal dos Sirionó." *Revista de Antropologia*
    –68   *de Sao Paulo* 1:16.
    1983   *Gejagte Jäger.* Teil 2. Die Mbia in Ostbolivien. Museum
            fur Volkerkunde Frankfurt am Main.

Meggers, Betty
    1971   *Amazonia: Man and Culture in a Counterfeit Paradise.*
            Chicago: Aldine.

Métraux, Alfred
    1942   *The Native Tribes of Eastern Bolivia and Western Matto
            Grosso.* Bureau of American Ethnology, bulletin no. 134.
    1963   "Tribes of Eastern Bolivia and the Madeira Headwaters."
            In Handbook of South American Indians, ed. Julian
            Steward. Bureau of American Ethnology, bulletin 143.
            New York: Cooper Square Publishers.

Needham, Rodney
    1954   "Sirionó and Penan: A Test of Some Hypotheses."
            Southwestern Journal of Anthropology 10:228–32.
    1961   "An Analytical Note on the Structure of Sirionó Society."
            Southwestern Journal of Anthropology 17:239–55.
    1964   "Descent, Category and Alliance in Sirionó Society."
            Southwestern Journal of Anthropology 10:229–40.

Nordenskiöld, Erland
    1917   "The Guaraní Invasion of the Inca Empire in the Six-
            teenth Century: An Historical Indian Migration."
            Geographical Review 4:103–21.

Orbigny, Alcide d'
    1893   *Voyage dans l'Amérique Méridionale.* Vol. 4, pt. 1,
            "L'Homme Américain (de l'Amérique Méridionale)."
            Paris.

"The Panare—Scenes from the Frontier."
1982   Produced by Melissa Llewellyn-Davies for the BBC.

Parejas, Alcides
1980   *Historia del Oriente Boliviano: Siglos XVI, XVII.* Santa Cruz: Universidad Gabriel René Moreno.

Priest, Anne
1964   "Method of Naming among the Sirionó Indians." Brief communications, *American Anthropologist.* 66:1149–51.

Priest, Perry
1980   *Estudios Sobre el Idioma Sirionó.* Notas de Bolivia, no. 10. Riberalta, Bolivia: Instituto Lingüistico de Verano.
1982   Personal communication.

Priest, Perry, and Anne Priest
1980   *Textos Sirionó.* Riberalta, Bolivia: Instituto Lingüistico de Verano.

Riester, Jürgen
1976   *En Busca de la Loma Santa.* La Paz, Bolivia: Amigos del Libro.

Rydén, Stig
1941   *A Study of the Sirionó Indians.* Goteborg: Elanders Boktyckeri Aktiebolag.

Sanabria, Fernando
1973   *Breve Historia de Santa Cruz.* La Paz: Librería Editorial "Juventud."

Scheffler, Harold W., and Floyd G. Lounsbury
1971   *A Study in Structural Semantics: The Sirionó Kinship System.* Englewood Cliffs, NJ: Prentice-Hall.

Shapiro, Warren
1968   "Kinship and Marriage in Sirionó Society: A Reexamination." *Bijdragen Tot de Taal-, Land-, en Volkerkunde* 124:40–55.

Stearman, Allyn MacLean
1984   "The Yuquí Connection: Another Look at Sirionó Deculturation." *American Anthropologist.* 86:630–50.

Steinbeck, John
1962   *Travels with Charley: In Search of America.* The Viking Press. New York. (Quotation is from page 4.)

Stoll, David
1982   *Fishers of Men or Founders of Empire?* London: Cultural Survival, Inc., Zed Press.

REFERENCES

Wegner, Richard N.

1928 "Die Quruñgu'a, ein Neuentdeckter Stamm Primitivister Kultur Ohne Artikulierte und Grammatikalische Sprache in Ostbolivien." *Phoneis, Zeitschrift Deutsche Geistersarbeit für Sudamerika.* Jahrgang 14, Hefts 4 and 5 p. 369–84.

1931 *Zum Sonnentor Durch Altes Indianerland.* Darmstadt.

1932 "Ostbolivianische Urwaldstamme." *Ethnologischer Anzeiger* 2:321–40.

1934 "Die Quruñgu'a und Sirionó." *International Congress of Americanists Proceedings* 24:161–84.